DNO *the* SEO
REVOLUTION

A Detailed Guide For Achieving Permanent
Page-One Rankings For UNDER $100

Robert McAnderson

New York

DNO *the* SEO REVOLUTION
A Detailed Guide For Achieving Permanent Page-One Rankings For UNDER $100

by **Robert McAnderson**

© 2012 Robert McAnderson. All rights reserved.

ISBN 978-1-61448-069-3 Paperback
ISBN 978-1-61448-070-9 eBook
Library of Congress Control Number: 2011932075

Published by:
MORGAN JAMES PUBLISHING
The Entrepreneurial Publisher
5 Penn Plaza, 23rd Floor
New York City, New York 10001
(212) 655-5470 Office
(516) 908-4496 Fax
www.MorganJamesPublishing.com

Cover Design by:
Rachel Lopez
rachel@r2cdesign.com

Interior Design by:
Bonnie Bushman
bbushman@bresnan.net

In an effort to support local communities, raise awareness and funds, Morgan James Publishing donates one percent of all book sales for the life of each book to Habitat for Humanity.
Get involved today, visit
www.HelpHabitatForHumanity.org.

ACKNOWLEDGMENTS

A special thanks to my life partner, business partner, wife, and the mother of our three beautiful daughters, Jacqui Gibbs-McAnderson, for listening to my endless prattle on the subject of SEO, SEM, and Google. At the beginning of this journey, she admitted to all who would listen that she just did not understand how these technologies worked. Today, however, she is no longer a student but master of social marketing and the contribution this marketing discipline makes to page-one rankings.

Jacqui struggled with the passion I have for internet strategies and the endless hours I spent testing my theories. When the idea started to take shape, and I was able to articulate my ideas more clearly, she became an avid supporter. As my business partner, she always wanted to know the answer to that question all business managers ask: "What is the ROI (return on investment) going to be and when will it be realized?"

To my three daughters, Courtney, Taylor, and Paige, thank you for your patience and for allowing me the time to indulge my desire to perfect this strategy. Your love and support is much appreciated.

TABLE OF CONTENTS

PREFACE

by Robert McAnderson

Website owners the world over know the power of a page-one Google ranking. That's why they spent a staggering **23.6 billion dollars** with Google in 2009 to buy this prime piece of real estate.

Taking into consideration the additional revenues from Yahoo, MSN/Bing, AltaVista, SEO(search engine optimization) software, SEO outsourced services, and SEM (search engine marketing) services, this number is a staggering **50-billion-dollar** industry dedicated to achieving page-one rankings.

There are two amazing facts associated with this **50-billion-dollar** spend. The results are **temporary** and, secondly, the cost of maintaining a page-one ranking increases by **20 percent** every year.

To replace any of the top-ten page-one ranked entities on Google requires only one action, your willingness to pay more than they have in the first instance. To maintain the ranking thereafter, you will be required to defend your position by continually outbidding your competitor, regardless of cost.

The strategy outlined in this book focuses on a systematic approach to acquiring a page-one ranking for less than $100 and being able to defend this ranking with minimal effort for decades.

The thought process behind the creation of this strategy started in early 2008, when I was working with a number of clients who wanted a page-one Google ranking. What I found interesting was all of these clients had professional-looking websites, but when I searched using the keywords critical to their product/service offering, I found it difficult if not impossible to find them.

When I ran SEO software over these websites, I was astonished at how poorly many of them rated; and when I searched some of the domain names on Google by placing their domain names in parentheses, I was unable to find a significant number of them. At this point, I thought I had discovered a lucrative marketing opportunity and the ability to use my SEO software to open discussions with prospective clients. What I found, however, was that a significant number understood the concept of SEO, but very few understood what was required to achieve a page-one Google ranking.

I knew the strategy had to be simple, capable of being used by both experienced and inexperienced users, deliver results and be resistant to changes made by the search engines to their page-ranking formulas in the future.

As the strategy started to take shape, I experimented with the On the Mark Marketing website until it became apparent I needed a better test site and the ability to monitor the outcomes of my experiments. At this time, I was running an extensive Google AdWords campaign originally designed by an SEM (search engine marketing) specialist, which I had assumed control of and had made numerous modifications to, resulting in a considerable improvement in the CTR (click-through rate) and had managed to reduce the CPC (cost per click).

AdWords provided one of the research tools I used to refine On the Mark Marketing's Google AdWords campaign, while providing an increasing awareness of the importance of the keyword search phrases used by internet surfers to find the products and services they were looking for.

Once proven, the next-biggest decision was how to market the strategy. I considered developing it into a software program, offering it as a fully outsourced service offering to a select number of highly targeted companies, or creating an e-book. The problem with all of these models was that they were time and resource critical; limited in their reach, and the internet strategy was capable of being stolen or claimed by others.

The idea of publishing the strategy as a book was a model that provided the widest distribution method and the ability for SME (small medium enterprise) businesses to compete on equal terms with their larger competitors. For the first time, it is about the ability of individuals to see the value of the strategy and how quickly they can take advantage of the opportunity rather than the size of their marketing budget.

I believe the internet strategy outlined in this book will have a monumental impact on the search engine optimization, search engine marketing, pay per click and search engine industries.

Overnight, the concept that has so heavily underpinned the methodology used by every SEO company will become obsolete. This industry will literally have to reinvent itself using the internet strategy outlined in the book or find creative variations to the theme that will put them back in the game.

SEO companies that choose to offer my internet strategy will be unable to survive on the dramatically reduced income from each SEO job, while also being unable to find enough customers to justify the continuation of their business.

SEM companies will struggle with the concept because of the additional competition a page-one Google ranking will force onto them. They will more than likely want to jump on board with the DNO internet strategy concept because it will increase the effectiveness of their programs. On the down side, click fraud is likely to become a bigger issue, and it will be harder for their customers to identify where sales leads are coming from. Clearly, Google would be the source of most of the leads, but determining if they came from AdWords or from the generic SEO top-ten listing will be difficult.

It is likely SEM and PPC will be scaled back as the SEO top-ten internet strategy starts to impact performance of these programs.

Finally, Google, Bing, Yahoo and the other search engines will dislike this internet strategy intensely because it challenges the stranglehold they have had on the market for the past ten years.

Chapter One

HOW TO BUILD
WEBSITE TRAFFIC

Whatever you have read in the past or now believe about creating website traffic—forget it if it does not focus on page rank and the relevance of your website copy compared to the keywords imbedded in your site's metadata. Search engines rank websites based on this relevance for one fundamentally simply rule: the websites they list for each keyword search have to be the ten most relevant websites. This simple rule but complicated assessment process is responsible for Google skyrocketing to market dominance in the search engine marketplace, and it is what will keep them there for many years to come.

If your website does not appear on page one when you search the keyword your target audience would use to find the goods or services you offer, then you need to take steps to address this situation urgently. Having said that, you need to be mindful that every other website owner in your market segment is trying to do the same thing. So you need to make sure you do it better or, perhaps as this book may provide a way to, do it smarter.

On any Google search results page, you will see twenty websites displayed. Ten paid to be there as part of their Google AdWords program, and they are ranked in the order based on one principal only—who paid the most to be there. The remaining ten websites are there because Google's page rank methodology ranks them as the ten most relevant websites on the internet for the searched keyword.

The Google AdWords subscribers appear across the top of the screen and down the right-hand side. The ranked position of these ten advertisers can change from hour to hour based on how much each advertiser is prepared to pay to stay on page one and in as high a ranked position as possible. This can change if the advertiser has set a daily budget that has been reached or if Google determine they are likely to generate a higher income from another advertiser by elevating them into a higher position. On any given day and at any specified time, the advertiser may choose to turn their AdWords campaign off in order to stay within the specific budget guidelines they have determined.

With an unlimited budget, any advertiser can stay in the number-one position for as long as they want. What many people do not understand is the PPC (pay per click) price advertisers actually pay, compared to their bid price for that keyword, can be substantially lower. You will find more on this subject along with some practical advice in Chapter Three: Pay-Per-Click Marketing.

To ensure advertisers maintain their ranked position in the top-ten advertisers and on page one, they need to monitor the price being paid for each keyword daily, possibly even hourly. If a competitor decides to increase their bid price on a keyword, the only possible response would be to bid a higher price in order to stay in the top position. Some advertisers use dedicated software, designed to identify how much a competitor is paying for their keywords, and to flag changes in ranked position when a competitor increases their bid price.

If you go to Google and search for the keywords "adwords management software," you will find several products to help measure, monitor, and control your campaign.

To be fair to Google, they do not want to be charging your credit card higher and higher fees every month and take them back to Ireland, where they pay the smallest company tax rate in the world. They genuinely want to help you manage your account, and so they provide ways to reduce monthly charges by allowing advertisers to turn off their campaigns at certain times of the day or on certain days of the week. Their theory being if the volume of traffic on the weekend is low, you could turn Saturday and Sunday off or, in instances where the volume of traffic between 2:00 am and 6:00 am is low, you could turn off the AdWords campaign during these times. They also allow advertisers to place a limit on their daily spend, and once this limit has been reached, the campaign is stopped automatically until the next day.

Wait a minute—if the number of people searching for my keywords is small on the weekend and between the hours of 2:00 am and 6:00 am Monday to Friday, how would turning my campaign off on these occasions help reduce my costs? As for placing a daily limit on my spend, all that does is give my competitors the website traffic and business leads that would normally have come to my website.

Surrendering my page-one AdWords position because I reached my daily spending limit gives my competitors potential business that could have been mine, and the confidence to expand their AdWords campaign, resulting in a more aggressive bidding war for the keywords that are so fundamental to my website's success.

The only winner from this activity is Google, whose revenues continue to rise a staggering 20 percent each year because business owners the world over keep bidding higher and higher prices for the keywords in their AdWords campaigns.

Okay, so you don't have an unlimited budget and you do not want your margins continuously squeezed to support a paid advertising campaign. Then you are going to need to be one of the ten SEO websites listed by the search engines as the most relevant websites for the keywords searched.

Performing an SEO function on your website is one option you should consider, so finding a reputable SEO company to improve your SEO ranking should be high on the list of things to do. Importantly, if you do not have several thousand dollars to spend on an SEO program and want to find out more about what you can do yourself to improve this ranking, then read on.

Detailed below is a list of things you need to do as soon as possible and an extended list of inclusions you need to incorporate into your website over time.

While I encourage you to incorporate each of these considerations to ensure you have a well-constructed website, the internet strategy outlined in this book will ensure you achieve a top-ten search engine ranking within weeks without having to incorporate all of them into your website. You don't need to do them all, so some of the more complex ones can be left until after you have a page-one ranking and can afford to fund them from profits generated from the internet strategy in this book.

1. Metadata Tags

Webpages need to include metadata in the form of metatags that provide a webpage title, a detailed description of the webpage, and a list of the keywords used to describe the webpage's content. Search engines use this metadata when adding pages to their search index. As part of this process, they compare the metatags with the page content to ensure the page is what it reports to be.

To maintain its dominance of the search engine market, Google is continuously modifying the process used to evaluate which websites to promote to its users as most relevant to the keywords they searched. This approach to servicing the needs of their visitors propelled them to become the largest search engine company in the world, replacing Yahoo within two years as the market leader—a position they have maintained ever since.

To give you some insight into what metadata should look like, I have included an example from the home page of our website www.onthemark.com.au. Importantly, metadata should be different for each page of your website, allowing the search engines to include a number of pages from your website in their top ten listings.

Title: Marketing consultants and rapid business builders —internet marketing, marketing strategies, sales strategies, branding strategies.

Description: Marketing consultants Sydney—Rapid business builders offering free marketing materials, pre-paid marketing, internet strategies, marketing strategies, sales strategies, branding strategies, and marketing for SME businesses.

Keywords: on the mark marketing, marketing consultants sydney, rapid business builders, internet marketing, internet strategies, marketing strategies, sales strategies, branding strategies, outsource marketing, free marketing materials, pre-paid marketing, sme businesses, marketing advice.

Robots: The robots metatag provides an instruction, such as "index,follow," to instruct the robots to index each page linked throughout your website. It is also possible to instruct the robots not to crawl your website or specific directories and website pages.

If you are not sure about the metadata on your website, then you can go to http://www.submitexpress.com/analyzer/. Enter your domain name and click on the "submit" button. The website will display for you the metadata for your domain name home page. If there is no metadata, then I suggest you arrange very quickly to add the metadata before submitting your website to the search engines. Oh, and just in case you haven't caught onto the point yet, the metadata needs to be different for each page on your website.

As an example, if you searched the keywords "rapid business builders" on www.google.com.au, you would see the metatags for the page description displayed on the Google page (see Diagram 1). After clicking the link, Google opens the site, and you can see the title of the webpage displayed in the Windows Explorer tab (see Diagram 2).

Diagram 1

Diagram 2

2. Search Engine Spiders

A search engine spider is a computer program designed to browse the World Wide Web in a methodical, automated fashion as a means of providing up-to-date data on all websites in its database. Web spiders create a text-based copy of all the visited pages for later processing and indexes the downloaded pages to provide fast searches. Spiders are used for maintenance tasks on a website, such as checking links, validating HTML code, and to gather specific types of information about webpages. In general, starting with a list of URLs to visit, called the seeds, the spider visits these URLs, identifying all the hyperlinks in the webpage, and adds them to the list of URLs to be visited. These URLs are recursively visited, according to a set of policies defined by the spider and from instructions included in the metatags on each website.

If your website has no metatags and has not been crawled by a search engine spider, then the chances of anyone finding your website on the internet is zero.

3. Use Keywords in Hyperlinks

Spiders look for links on your website that contain hyperlinks that include the keywords used in your metatags. The search engines assess the relevance of each webpage to all of the other websites in your market segment and regional location based on this consideration. As an example, the keyword phrase "<u>internet strategies</u>" is included in our keyword metadata, appears as a keyword phrase on the content of our home page, and is hyperlinked to a separate page on our website that contains content relevant to internet strategies.

4. Use Keywords in Filenames

Similarly, it is important to use the keywords as a means of identifying linked webpages and other downloadable content. As an example, the use of the keyword phrase "internet strategies" for On the Mark Marketing is shown as <u>http://www.onthemark.com.au/internet_strategies.htm</u>

5. Submit the Website to the Major Search Engines

If you have not already done so, then you need to submit your website to the major search engines so they can crawl your website and regularly update the data they store about your website.

You can start by submitting your website to the following major search engines.

<u>http://www.google.com.au/addurl/?continue=/addurl</u>
<u>http://www.bing.com/webmaster/SubmitSitePage.aspx</u>
<u>http://siteexplorer.search.yahoo.com/submit</u>

Submissions to Bing automatically flow through to ninemsn, while Yahoo flows through to AltaVista.

If you have not already done this or had someone do it for you, then you are the proud owner of a website that no one will ever be able to find using a search engine. If you want to test if you are in the search engine database, then simply type "www.YourDomainName.com.au," making sure you use the parentheses on either side of the URL, into Google and see if your domain name is displayed. Interestingly, this will also tell you how many external links there are on other websites that link to your domain name.

6. Social Media Like Twitter, Facebook

Social media is becoming a very important component for generating website traffic and elevating the ranking of websites. Links between social media and webpages contribute to the ranking process by building the keyword values of the various webpages. The ability to attract visitors from social media websites, publish comments, measure trends, and product acceptance via this forum can be valuable information to help you understand your target audience's interests and requirements.

Importantly, the ability to communicate with your followers and the people who follow them increases the distribution of your message by a factor of ten.

From a Twitter perspective, I have taken the time to build a good network of over 10,000 followers. This provides me with an opportunity to communicate not only with these 10,000 people, but also—in many instances—to all of *their* followers.

From a Facebook perspective, my wife Jacqui launched a marketing campaign in March 2011 using a purposefully built Facebook application designed to attract and then engage an audience. It started with a small gift on March 3rd to 20,000 people in every capital city of Australia, and within a week, the

Facebook application had almost 11,000 followers. Further, it had engaged over 80 percent of the wholesale industry that supplied specialty products to the 500 retailers who registered to participate in the program. The Facebook application simply asked the Facebook friend to enter the postcode where they live. They are then presented with a map listing the full contact details of every retailer in that postcode carrying stock and who is part of the program.

If you are interested and would like to see how effective this has been, then go to http://www.facebook.com/plantlifebalance and see for yourself.

Social media marketing has come of age, so if it's not part of your current media mix, you need to give some thought to making it part.

7. Blogs

Blogs predate the development of social media, such as Facebook, MySpace, and Twitter. They are an excellent forum for communicating ideas and opinions because there are no limitations to the amount of text that can be used and because they can be indexed and maintained online indefinitely.

Because blogs build links to your website, search engines regard them strongly. For this reason alone, there is considerable value in developing and maintaining a blog on your website.

8. Published Articles and Deep Links

There are a number of websites that will allow you to publish articles on the internet. You don't need to be a professional copywriter, but having the ability to write short, valuable information directed at your target audience would be very helpful.

People who are looking for ideas and inspiration frequently visit these websites, copy the articles, and use them on other websites.

These website are highly regarded by search engines because of the volume of traffic they attract. The benefit to any author who publishes an article on one of these websites is the deep links back to your website. In instances where articles are copied and used on other websites, the link from these websites adds to your page's page rank.

While there are a number of these article-based websites, I have chosen to list two I have found easy to use. I recommend you have a look at them and consider developing articles for publication on these websites. Importantly, also publish these articles on your blog and use Twitter and Facebook to increase their exposure.

www.hubpages.com
www.articlebase.com

9. Publish a Regular Newsletter

Communication is king when building relationships with current and potential customers, and the development of a regular newsletter is one way of building website traffic.

The style of the newsletter should be short and punchy, offering a précis of the article with a link back to your website where a full version of the news item can be found. Newsletters should contain a précis of a number of articles and some information about you and your company.

Articles need to reflect what your customers and potential clients want to read and be informed about and should be produced once a month.

In the past few years, we have seen great acceptance of HTML newsletters by marketers, which leads to the inboxes of many recipients being jammed to capacity. This results in a decreasing number of e-mails that are actually being read. Technology providers recognizing these trends have developed smarter solutions designed to increase readership and identify those recipients who have read the newsletter.

Go to Google and search the term "e-mail marketing software" for a list of possible suppliers.

I have included links to three of these organizations that offer e-mail newsletter generation and tracking. Take the time to have a look at these websites and gain an understanding of what can be achieved with this technology.

http://www.emailmarketingsoftware.com.au/
www.email-marketing.simplycast.com
www.vision6.com.au/

Some of you will be comfortable with writing your own materials and have little difficulty in turning out material and articles that will be of interest to your current and future customers. If you are not one of these people, then the answer is to hire someone who has the skills to do it for you, but importantly, don't let your inability in this area be an obstacle to developing this material.

10. Autoresponders

When a visitor to your website requests information, he or she expects a quick response. I know from my experience I will jump from my internet browser to my e-mail system immediately after making a request or purchase to look for the response.

Autoresponders are essential today and help build relationships and meet expectations. From a website traffic perspective, do not fall into the trap of allowing the requester or customer who has just made a purchase to navigate to a webpage where the materials can be found. Rather, put a link to the page into your auto-responder e-mail, ensuring the visitor clicks one more time onto your website.

Remember, traffic is king.

11. RSS Feeds

RSS (really simple syndication) feeds will push content from several different websites of interest to the website reader.

An RSS document ("feed," "web feed," or "channel") includes full or summarized text, plus metadata, such as publishing dates and authorship. Web feeds benefit the publishers by letting them syndicate content automatically. Readers benefit from the subscription to timely updates from their favored websites or the convenience to aggregate feeds from many sites into one place.

RSS feeds can be read using software called an "RSS reader," "feed reader," or "aggregator," which can be web based, desktop based, or mobile-device based. A standardized XML file format allows the information to be published once and viewed by many different programs. The user subscribes to a feed by entering into the reader the feed's URL or by clicking an RSS icon in a web browser that initiates the subscription process.

The RSS reader checks the user's subscribed feeds regularly for new work, downloads any updates that it finds, and provides a user interface to monitor and read the feeds. RSS allows users to avoid manually inspecting all of the websites they are interested in, and instead subscribe to many websites such that all new content is pushed onto their browsers when it becomes available.

12. PPC Marketing

Pay-per-click or PPC marketing, as it is also known, is a simple process that allows you to generate website traffic based on a selection of keywords. Users of the system bid for prominent placement on search engines, such as Google, Bing, and Yahoo.

Behind each keyword is a user-developed advert designed to attract the reader's attention, encouraging them to click on the link. This concept has been explained in detail in Chapter Three.

13. Webinars

Webinars are essentially PowerPoint presentations delivered online using a web conferencing service. They are an increasingly popular way to present educational and white-paper-like content. They are common in the technology industry but underused in many other market segments. Webinars give your message the combined impact of audio, visuals, and interactivity. However, they do tie your audience to their computers for thirty to sixty minutes.

14. Podcasts

Audio podcasts can be almost any length and are used for a variety of purposes, from creating an interest-generating "teaser" to an audio white paper. "Podcast" is actually a misnomer; these audio segments should be called "netcasts," as most executives listen to them at their desks. While podcasts lack the visual component of webinars, they give your content wings, freeing your recipient from the computer; once downloaded to an MP3 player, a podcast can be listened to on a plane, in a cab, or while working out at the gym. While you can record a podcast using various software packages or web services, unless you're an expert, it's best to hire a podcasting specialist to edit out the pauses, "ums," and "ahs," and assure that your podcast is produced and promoted effectively and professionally.

15. Google PageRank

PageRank is a ranking between 0 and 10 with 10 being the highest ranking a page can receive. Essentially, the ranking is a vote of confidence in a website, with the higher PageRank being considered a more "trusted" website by Google.

PageRank (PR), in short, means the difference between life and death from a webmaster perspective. If you are trying to build a commerce website that generates substantial revenues with loads of daily visitors, PageRank should feature strongly in your thinking.

How to Get a High Google PageRank

The single most effective way to achieve a high PageRank is to write quality content; it's that simple and it's that complex. Secondly, PageRank relies heavily on links, incoming and outgoing links are a major factor in your website's PageRank. Every link that comes into your site is given a value. The overall value of your incoming links weighs heavily on your Google PageRank.

Every link is assigned a value based on how high the site that is linked to you is rated. For example, 1,000 inbound links from websites that don't have a PageRank will not rank as highly as 100 links from websites with a PR5.

There are also factors that you cannot control when it comes to PR. The older your site, the more trusted it becomes, and therefore it is looked upon more favorably by Google. Google wants lots of pages, lots of incoming links, and lots of internal links. That means that you should try to link to as many pages inside your site as possible. This should not be hard because it only helps your cause.

Some website owners even buy incoming links from sites with a high Google PR.

For more details on how PageRank works, refer to Chapter Six.

Chapter Two

KEYWORD RESEARCH

After reviewing thousands of websites to determine their visibility on the internet, I have come to one inexhaustible conclusion: there are many website developers who have the talent to develop professional-looking, easy-to-navigate websites, but have no idea about the value of keywords. I have seen websites without any keywords, the wrong keywords, and finally one website where the keywords had more to do with the content-managed software and the website developer than they did about the website itself.

I have run SEO reports on many of these websites and been appalled to find the metadata is mismatched to the page content, as were the keywords (if there were any) to the products and services being offered.

From a website development perspective, I have met with thousands of SME business owners who see the necessity of a website but are not prepared to invest more than four to five thousand dollars developing one. So, why should it be a surprise to anyone that the only purpose many of these websites serve is to act as an online company brochure for existing customers and specific prospects who, through direct sales efforts, have become aware of the website's existence. Prospective customers who use the internet to find a supplier of the goods and services they are looking to purchase will never view these websites.

For any website to be successful, the business owner, as well as the website developer, has to understand the importance of keywords. After all, keywords are the method a prospective customer uses to find websites amongst the hundreds of millions published on the internet.

Website copy needs to be informative and contain a compelling reason for the visitor to stay on the site longer, navigate to other pages, and ultimately become convinced to buy a product or services. It is imperative website developers spend time trying to get inside the head of their typical customer and to identify the keywords he or she uses when searching for the products or services offered. They need to incorporate these keywords into the website's metadata, webpage title, description, and keywords, as well as the website's page content. Keyword density must be somewhere between five percent and ten percent, any higher and the search engines will subtract points from your ranking, any lower and the website will not be regarded as relevant by the search engines.

Search engines use spiders to crawl all known websites on the internet and update their search engine databases from the metadata found in each website while measuring this metadata against the content of the webpage, forming a page ranking in part based on keyword relevance. To gain a page-one ranking, Google's page ranking methodology must rank the webpage as one of the ten most relevant webpages on the internet. For a detailed explanation about how PageRank works, go to Chapter Six, "Understanding Google's Market Dominance and How Their Ranking Works." However, the following simple explanation will tell you what you can change quickly and inexpensively.

If you are not sure if your website contains metadata or its relevance to webpage content, go to the following free online analytical tool, enter your website's home page URL, and click on the "submit" button. This website will deliver in seconds a detailed assessment of your webpage and how the search engine spider assesses the relevance of your webpages. http://www.submitexpress.com/analyzer/

The simple report will highlight the metadata for title, description, and content, ranking out of one hundred the relevance of the metadata to the content on the page. While it is possible to get one hundred percent relevance in each category, anything less than eighty percent should warrant your urgent attention.

Run the same test for several of your website's pages and make sure the ranking is above eighty percent for each webpage. If the same metadata has been used on all of the webpages, then you need to make changes quickly if you want these pages to be searchable in their own right. Remember, the ideal position is to occupy two or more slots of the top ten pages on page one of all the search engines because it simply doubles the chances of your website generating business.

If you want to find out how your website is currently ranked, then go to the following free online website, enter your home page URL, and see how well your website ranks against other websites for the same keywords. Do not enter any competitive website or add your e-mail address unless you want this company to follow you up offering to perform an SEO function on your website. The report will confirm many of the points I have raised in the book and is a yardstick for measuring the effectiveness of any changes you make to your website in the future. http://websitegrader.com/

The number of times the keywords are found in the metadata and webpage content as plain text, bold text, or H1 to H6 heading tags contributes to the PageRank. Spiders see the H-tags and bold text as headlines that relate to the content published on the webpage and use these elements to determine page relevancy. Metadata keywords, page title, page description, H-tags, and bold text followed by relevant content, internal hyperlinks, and links from other highly regarded websites confirms the webpage is what it purports to be, and thereafter is ranked against every other webpage for the same keyword.

Given the search engine spider returns to your website based on the invitation found in the robots metadata, the frequency of changes made to the website, or a combination of both of these factors, the need to constantly measure websites performance against other websites you compete against is essential to retaining a page-one ranking from an SEO perspective.

The creation of inbound and outbound links incorporating the same keywords is important if they link to other websites or internal pages where the content is similarly measured for its relevance. Therefore, when constructing the naming conventions of each page of your website, ensure the page URL contains the keyword. As an example, the keyword phrase "internet strategies" has been incorporated into the page URL of the On the Mark Marketing website as follows: http://www.onthemark.com.au/internet_strategies.htm.

Social media, such as Twitter, Facebook, YouTube, and blogs, has come to play a more and more important part in this equation. You will have noticed this importance if you have visited http://websitegrader.com/and performed the simple online test outlined earlier in this chapter. Individual rankings for Twitter, Facebook, blogs, and RSS contribute to the overall ranking of a webpage, while websites like YouTube provide links back to your homepage. While all of this is important, working the keywords into these links is vitally important.

High-ranking webpages appear on page one of Google because Google needs to deliver to search engine users websites with content considered to be the most relevant for the keyword searched. Bottom line, if your website is not on page one of Google, your website is unlikely to be found, and if you doubt this, then reflect on your own use of Google. From my perspective, if it is not on page one, I am not looking any further.

As we have discussed previously, page one of Google is broken into two sections: AdWords and the SEO section. Google has ranked the ten websites that appear in the SEO generic section as the ten most relevant websites on the internet for the specific keyword that was searched.

What better place to start when developing or redeveloping a website other than a research tool that will tell you every keyword searched on Google for the past twelve months broken down into your local region, internationally, while telling you how much the PPC was for that keyword.

Research Tools

If you don't already have a Google AdWords account, sign up for one now by going to https://www.google.com/accounts. You don't have to use this account or run a Google AdWords campaign, nor do you have to pay Google for the privilege of setting up the account.

Once established, and you have logged in, click on the "reporting and tools" tab and then the "keyword tool" link in the dropdown box, as shown in Diagram 3.

Diagram 3

In the "word or phrase (one per line)" window, type a keyword or phrase that best describes one of your products or services. If you have multiple keywords or phrases for the same product or service, enter them on the following line but do not mix products or services.

Importantly, do not enter your website details in the second window; instead, leave this window blank.

Google will present a list of keywords along with the number of times each keyword was searched globally and locally last month and the past twelve months.

Click on the "download" tab and then "all," as shown in Diagram 4. A dropdown list of different file formats is displayed. The selection options default to "CSV for Excel." Assuming you use Excel, click the "download" button, and the system will download a comprehensive Excel spreadsheet containing all of the details for the keyword or phrases displayed on screen.

Diagram 4

Once you have this information in an Excel spreadsheet, click on the sort button and sort the entire spreadsheet by the column titled "local monthly searches," highest to lowest.

You now have a list of all the keywords or phrases searched for in your region, ranked most-frequently searched to least-frequently searched.

Repeat this function for any additional keywords or phrases that best describe other products or services your company sells, combining each Excel outcome into a worksheet "sheet" tab in the same spreadsheet. Once you have completed the process for all the keywords and phrases, rename each of the tabs with the keywords or phrases.

Importantly, some of the keywords or phrases in this spreadsheet will have no relevance to you; it's simply Google's way of encouraging you to use more keywords in your AdWords campaign in the hope of generating more PPC revenue. If some of the keywords are not applicable, delete them.

The information you have details the keywords your customers use when searching for your products and services. It's an invaluable source of information that details how your customers think when searching on the internet. Analyzing these keywords to determine how each of them can be used on your website is critical to the website's development and PageRank.

Google Insights

Effectively takes the same information generated by Google's Keyword Tool, and shows how the keywords used by internet users searching for product/services have changed over time. Additionally, the process charts the rise and evolution of keywords you have targeted while showing the location in the world where these keywords have been used most. Seasonal and trends analysis will improve keywords selection contributing to higher page one rankings.

Google Insights is well hidden on the Google website in fact you have to navigate to the Reporting and Tools tab and select the option at the bottom of the drop down selection called, *More Tools*. Clicking on the More Tools option navigates to a new page and at the bottom left hand side of the list you will see the Google Insights tool.

http://www.google.com/insights/search will take you directly to the Google Insights page.

Using Google Insights is relatively simple. The examples below showcase some different ways of using Google *Insights for Search*. Whether you're an advertising agency, a small business owner, a multinational corporation, or an academic researcher, *Insights for Search* can help you gauge interest in pertinent search terms.

Insights can also help you determine which messages resonate best with your target audience. For example, an automobile manufacturer may be unsure of whether to highlight **fuel efficiency**, **car safety**, or **engine performance** to market a new car model. Diagram 5 illustrates that between 2004 and the present day **car safety** ranks high in the consumer's mind followed by **engine performance** and last of all **fuel efficiency**.

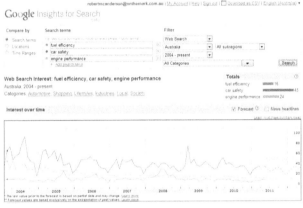

Diagram 5

Diagram 6 illustrates a notable shift in the importance of keywords when the time filter is changed from 2004 to the present day, to the last 12-months.

DNO *the* **SEO REVOLUTION**

Diagram 6

Diagram 7 shows a pattern of interest over all the states of Australia for Fuel Efficiency.

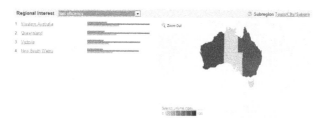

Diagram 7

Diagram 8 shows a pattern of interest over all the states of Australia for Car Safety.

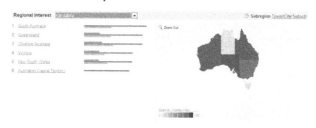

Diagram 8

Diagram 9 shows a pattern of interest over all the states of Australia for Engine Performance.

Diagram 9

Diagram 10 shows a drop down selection box showing further refinement of search terms used for under **car safety.** Knowing specifically what people are searching for when they use Google to find a product/service gives you a better chance of having them navigate to your website and converting this visit to sales.

Diagram 10

If you click on the "download as CSV" link at the top of the webpage the system will download a comprehensive Excel spreadsheet containing all of the details for the search terms used.

Save the Excel spreadsheet, as we will use this information later to assist in achieving a page-one ranking in fourteen days.

Use this information to construct webpages and landing pages for PPC AdWords campaigns that deliver what the website visitor is looking for. This information will prove to be invaluable for PPC, SEM, SEO, or any combination of these offerings, and will go a long way to delivering a page-one ranking and a significant increase in the volume of traffic to your website.

While the techniques outlined in this book will deliver a page-one ranking, you may still want to explore the SEM, SEO, or PPC options to give you some idea of the cost and timelines associated with these options. I have outlined the cost and timelines associated with these programs. In Australia, the lowest level of investment to implementing these options has been detailed in the table below.

Program	Initial Investment	Per Month	Per 3 Years
Pay-Per-Click	Nil	$700	$25,200
SEM	$1,500	$100	$5,100
SEO	$5,000	$500	$23,000
All Three	$6,5 00	$1,300	$53,300

The internet strategy outlined in this book will secure a page-one ranking within two weeks and will not require a PPC, SEM, or SEO investment. Your competitors will be unable to counter the internet strategies and will be forced to use one or more of the above programs. Be comforted in the knowledge it will cost them $700 a month to be on page one of Google and a further $700 every month to stay there. Know also that this cost **WILL** increase, as the competitors running AdWords campaigns outbid each other for the option of staying on page one of Google's AdWords.

Should any of your competitors implement an SEO program to increase their page-one ranking, it will cost them a minimum of $5,000 and take between three and six months to achieve the ranked result. Know also that in order to maintain this position, they will have to pay ten percent of that fee every month to stay there. They may also have to run a PPC campaign as part of an interim strategy while the SEO program slowly makes headway.

Importantly, rankings achieved through an SEO process can change at any time Google decides to change the way they rank websites. For this reason, and because multiple companies are competing for the same SEO ranking, anyone who starts an SEO process will have to maintain the process continuously to keep their SEO ranking.

Finally, and most importantly, the internet strategy outlined in this book will secure and maintain your SEO ranking because it uses techniques that leverage the founding principles Google uses to deliver content-rich websites to its user base, and these principals will never change. Be the first in your market to adopt the internet strategy and you can block every competitor in your market from following.

If you don't currently have a website and you are looking to develop one, the following comments may help you determine who you should engage to assist you in developing one.

Recently, I searched the term "website development process" on Google to determine what the industry considers the process to be. I was disappointed but not surprised to learn that only two of the top ten website developers made any reference to the use of keywords, and in both instances, the reference was casual.

The ten websites varied slightly in opinions, but all included the following: analysis, specifications, design and development, content development, code development, testing, promotion, and finally, maintenance and updating.

This traditional approached to website development is responsible for the creation of numerous first-class design concepts that are both easy to navigate and very informative for the visitor. They are also responsible for producing websites that are poorly ranked by the search engines or incapable of being found other than by their URL.

Only one of the websites promoted the concept of SEO (search engine optimization), and they recommended the process be started at the end of the website development process. For the life of me, I cannot understand why these so-called "specialists" recommend doing this work at the end of the development process, given this approach would require significant change to all the work performed at the first stage of the project.

This industry needs to re-evaluate its approach to website design. Throw away the traditional approach and start building websites from keyword research that confirm what search engine users actually use to find products/services using a search engine.

Keyword research should be used to help construct the URL page names, title, description, and the group of keywords associated with each page. From this point on, the content for the page should be developed along with graphics to support the keywords for each page of the website.

What I am proposing is the process be reversed by starting at the end and working towards the beginning rather than starting at the beginning and having to rework what you started with before you get to the end.

Chapter Three

PAY-PER-CLICK MARKETING

With a reported turnover from PPC advertising of 23.6 billion dollars in 2009, and every advertiser progressively bidding higher and higher PPC prices for their keywords, the cost effectiveness of these programs is starting to be questioned by many users.

Google, never at a loss to exploit the PPC growth opportunity, regularly sends e-mails to their AdWords account holders advising them of the need to increase their daily spending limits. They do this because their current spend is only running X percent of the time or the e-mail points out that by increasing the daily spend by X dollars, they will achieve an X percent increase in website visitors.

There is one central idea, one key concept that Google wants you to understand, and if you get this right, Google will reward you with lower prices per clicks while your number of new customers will grow incrementally. On the other hand, if you don't get it right, you will pay more than you have to per click. The one thing that matters to Google is relevance.

Google's mission is to build a search engine that gives people exactly what they are searching for, as fast as possible. If you are searching for "butterflies," they want to give you the very best and most popular butterfly websites on the very first page of results.

They have an amazing mathematical formula for figuring out who visited websites and why, and they use this formula as part of their PageRank process to deliver the most highly ranked webpages to search engine users.

When Google began to sell PPC AdWords advertising, they were concerned that advertisers needed to offer messages that were highly relevant to the keyword. Google rewards you for being relevant, and they let people who are searching vote for you. If your ad is clicked on, it is considered relevant. If not, it is not relevant—it is that simple.

The higher your click-through rate (CTR), i.e., the more people who see your ad and click on it, the less you have to pay for the position you want. But if you ads do not interest visitors, Google will make you pay more to display your ads.

What really matters is that your ads and your content be relevant to the keywords you are bidding on. Your message must match what the person is thinking when he or she uses a keyword to describe their requirements.

When you think about your product or service, you have to think about its relevance to the consumer who is using Google to find a supplier. If you can put yourself in the consumers' position and write ads that appeal to them, the number of clicks on your site will increase dramatically.

The price you bid is almost never the price you actually pay. Get it right and you will almost always pay less.

First, it's a little bit like eBay. You pay one cent above the next highest bid, not the maximum that you bid. But there is an even more important secret that is the key to getting lower and lower prices, even while other bidders are jumping into the game:

Your click-through rate (CTR) is more important than how much you bid. The click-through rate is the percentage of people searching who actually click on your ad. If one hundred people search, and your ad appears one hundred times, and one person clicks through, that is a one percent click-through rate. So, let's say I have a one percent CTR and I am paying $0.50 for position number two.

Now, let's say you have a two percent CTR. If you play your cards right, you may only have to pay $0.31 to get position number two and knock your competitor down to position number three.

That means that you were two times more relevant, and you only had to pay half as much!

The rules are very simple, but the implications are huge. When you achieve high click-through rates, you can pull your bid prices down and yet stay at the same position on the page, while your website traffic goes up.

The difference can be quite amazing. Here is an example of two ads—they are almost identical, but one got nearly twenty times the CTR as the other:

Sales Auditing
Let's Build Your Business Together.
We Are the Sales Auditing Experts
www.onthemark.com.au
One Click —CTR0.34 percent

Sales Auditing
We Are the Sales Auditing Experts
Let's Build Your Business Together.
www.onthemark.com.au
45 Clicks —CTR 4.44 percent

While both of these ads displayed the URL <u>www.onthemark.com.au</u>, both ads were directed to a landing page titled <u>www.onthemark.com.au/salesstrategy.htm</u>, which contained content regarded by Google as being highly relevant to the ad and the keyword searched.

Notice what happened: All that has changed is the reversal of two lines—and the click-through rate jumped from 0.34 percent to 4.44 percent!

That means that the second ad received more than forty five times the traffic of the first ad and, importantly, the cost per click (CPC) fell from AU$1.23 to a low AU$0.53. With a higher CTR resulting in increased website traffic, and at less than half the price, how can you go wrong?

Just think how much money you could be wasting on your Google AdWords campaign by not following some very logical advice. Push your bid prices down, down, down while your traffic goes up. By constantly changing your ad in an effort to beat older, better-performing ads, you can get more and more traffic for less.

Google ranks your ad higher as your CTR goes up, leaving those with more money than brains to subsidize the people who know how to make Google work for them.

Many Google AdWords customers simply increase the bid price of a keyword to maintain a current-ranked position. Apart from escalating the cost of the AdWords program, this approach will eventually result in the user pausing more and more keywords, because costs are increasing to a point where the user refuses to pay that high a price for someone to click on an ad.

One of the main reasons people don't purchase goods from your website or make contact to find out more about your offering is because the Google ad and the website landing page's content don't match what the person wanted when he or she typed the keyword into Google in the first instance.

As the old saying goes, "if it walks like a duck, sounds like a duck, can be found swimming in a pond, and has waterproof feathers, then it's likely to be a duck." So goes the argument for webpage relevance to the keyword. Apart from being what you say you are, you also have to be relevant to the selection of keywords aligned under each AdWords ad group. Find the right highly searched keywords, group them into ad groups, develop ads that are compelling to your target audience, and you will capture the imagination of the highest proportion of people searching for what you are really selling.

From my perspective, there is nothing worse than searching for a keyword and finding a Google ad that seems to meet my requirements, only to find when I click on the ad I am taken to a website that doesn't have what I was looking for. It's just a waste of time. eBay has a bad reputation for this when you search on Google; their ads suggest they have what you are looking for, but when you click on the ad, guess what, they really do not have one of those products.

How do you fix this problem? By organizing your keywords into narrow, targeted themes, by developing ads that motivate search engine users to click on your link because they believe you are offering what they need, and finally, by constantly testing different ads for each theme, trying to improve your CTR. The trick to perfecting this approach is by trying to leapfrog your highest-performing CTR ad while pausing the poorer-performing ads with low CTR.

So, a good place to start is with the keyword research you have collected from Google, as defined in Chapter Two, "Keyword Research."

To achieve the highest CTR and pay less than your bid price for each keyword, you will need to develop an effective PPC AdWords campaign that focuses on grouping similar keywords into specific groups called "ad groups," and then developing two different but similar ads around these keywords for each Ad Group. AdWords provides you with the ability to display a URL in your advertisement, which in the example shown is (www.OnTheMark. com.au), while having visitors who click on this ad directed to a specific landing page instead of the home page. In the example shown in Diagram 11 under column C is an ad group called "marketing strategies," and in this ad group, I have placed all the keywords relevant to this keyword phrase.

In order to achieve the highest conversion rate for this ad group, the visitor would land on the webpage www.onthemark. com.au/marketingstrategy.htm that has been developed specifically to provide information about marketing strategies.

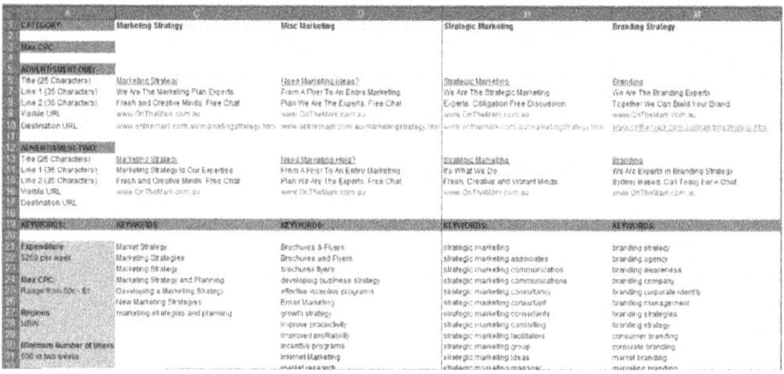

Diagram 11

Following this simple guideline will allow you to develop different AdWords ads for which the keywords have been clearly

defined and for which the same or similar keywords do not appear in two different columns. This is important because you do not want two different ads competing against each other in your AdWords campaign.

Make sure you feature the keyword phrase that was most searched according to your Google keyword research in the first line of the available 88 characters AdWords allows you to use for each ad. Develop a second ad using the first and second most searched keywords if possible, and let the public decide which ad is the most captivating.

Create a landing page for each AdWords ad by modifying an existing webpage or by developing a new one that incorporates these keyword phrases, ensuring the keywords appear in the metadata, H1 headings, bold text, hyperlinks, and webpage URLs.

Use the Excel spreadsheet to cut and paste copy into your AdWords account page. This will reduce the time it takes to create the various ad groups in your AdWords campaign while providing you with a permanent offline copy of what you have created.

Once you have created several ad groups for your AdWords campaign, just watch as search engine users vote by clicking on the words that actually sell. This is an absolutely foolproof method of getting your ads placed higher on the page. The reason for this is Google will always wrestle with the PPC revenue and the need on their part to deliver content-rich websites that match the search engine user's keyword.

The success of your AdWords campaign depends on the following:

- Your ability to select the right keywords.
- Breaking the keywords into narrow, targeted themes.

- Choosing enough keywords but not too many.
- Bidding low to start while monitoring performance.
- Developing multiple ads and always running two for each ad group.
- Replacing poor-performing ads with new ads to test market acceptance.
- Pausing old, poor-performing ads.
- Pausing keywords that don't work or have an unrealistic cost but not deleting them.
- Developing landing pages with content-rich copy for each targeted theme.
- Developing metatags for each landing page relevant to the page content and keyword targeted theme.
- Constantly measure and improve your AdWords campaign.
- Monitor keyword performance against the keyword file you downloaded from Google in the first instance.

The number-one mistake most people make is bidding on too few keywords. If you are bidding on less than twenty keywords, you will have a very hard time making it work. That's because the keywords that you are bidding on are the same ones everyone else is probably bidding on.

You should start with at least two hundred keywords broken into themes, each with a minimum of ten keywords. Remember, it is easier to start big, let the market downsize your selection by the choices people make, and pausing keywords rather than deleting them.

The following two documents produced by Google may help explain this a little further.

www.onthemark.com.au/AgencyOptimisationTips.pdf
www.onthemark.com.au/SearchEngineOptimization
StarterGuide.pdf

Online management of the campaign presents you with a raft of information about the number of times keywords are searched, the click-through rate, and what position your advertisement appears in the sponsored section of Google AdWords. Remember, the more traffic that comes to your website, the higher your ranking on page one is likely to be.

Google displays messages on the AdWords site that tell you what price you need to bid for each keyword in order to be on page one and provides a method of adding additional keywords to your campaign. Be careful the keywords you select fall within the theme of each campaign. It would be very easy to add keywords that fit across all of your campaigns into one themed for a specific range of ads, thus diluting the effectiveness of your program.

Assuming you are running a Google AdWords campaign, you should activate the Google Analytics reporting option. This requires you to add a little bit of code into the top header of your website and to confirm this with Google by having them test whether the code is present. Once up and running, the report will assist you in understanding how frequently people visit you website, what pages they navigate to, how long they stay on each page, where they come from, and what page they leave your website from. This information is a valuable asset that will help you improve website performance over time.

My PPC program with Google at one stage was costing me between $750 and $1,000 a month. To stay on top, I needed to be aware of what my competitors were paying for the same keywords and be prepared to outbid them in order to stay on top of the rankings. What started to happen was that I reached a point where I questioned whether the keyword was worth the cost I was paying for the website visit.

When keywords became too expensive, I just paused the keyword rather than pay $10 to get someone to click on my website. Ultimately, I found myself in the position where I could not justify paying higher and higher prices for the same keywords, so I put a limit on how much I was prepared to pay daily.

Google AdWords gives users the ability to run their campaigns during certain times of the day and night. Arguably, few people are searching the internet for marketing strategies between two and six in the morning, so concentrating my spend in the remaining hours sounded like a good idea. Alternatively, looking for patterns in CTR to determine other times during the day when my prospective customers were not searching the internet and my AdWords campaign could be turned off seemed like a good idea. Google also provides you with the ability to put a daily limit on your AdWords spend, and once reached, your ads just simply stop running.

The problem with all of these options is when potential customers are searching the internet, I need my ads running, so turning the AdWords campaign off when they're not searching for my products and services seems a little unproductive.

Similarly, putting a daily limit on my spending just meant I would attract potential customers during one part of the day, and during the remaining part of the day they would be directed to my competitors. Ultimately, the daily limit held my costs at an affordable level, but this limitation was a compromise I found hard to accept.

Google, in a predicable fashion, would post notifications on my Google AdWords account website that I was missing hundreds of visitors and I would need to increase my daily spend by thirty percent, then forty percent, and just before I suspended the account, fifty percent if I wanted the additional traffic.

The internet strategy outlined in the book will give every reader who employs the strategy a page-one ranking and the ability to be less reliant on AdWords, offering the potential to scale down and potentially cancel their PPC advertising, saving tens of thousands of dollars a year thereafter.

If you don't feel you have the skills to run an AdWords campaign, then you need to find yourself a professional search engine marketer who can set up and run your campaign for you.

Chapter Four

SEARCH ENGINE MARKETING

Google is cunning enough to know there are a number of Google AdWords users who don't understand how to set up and run AdWords in a way that will secure maximum results for the smallest investment, and to know that happy AdWords users contribute to stronger PPC annual growth. They offer SEM services directly to their customers and encourage others to setup SEM businesses as Google AdWords specialists, marketing Google to their existing and potential client bases.

Sometimes, the universe reaches out to you and just gives you exactly what you wanted. Right in the middle of typing the last paragraph, I received an e-mail from Google. Here it is for you to read and absorb; all I have changed is the voucher number.

Want new business online?

Increase visitors to your site with this introductory **$50 Google AdWords free trial**.

Do you want your business to stand out from competition?

Google AdWords can place your advertising message in front of potential customers at the exact time they're searching on Google. Using keywords—specific words you choose that relate to your business—your ad can show up as a "sponsored link" alongside Google search results for related products or services.

Tens of thousands of Australian businesses are already using Google AdWords. Here is why:

- **It's targeted:** Your ads only appear to people searching for terms relevant to your business. This $50 free trial could attract 100 new visitors to your site, assuming an average cost-per-click of 50 cents.*
- **It's affordable:** AdWords works even with small budgets. You can cap your daily spend (e.g., $10.00 a day) and only pay when potential customers click on your ad. Even better, you decide how much each click is worth to you and AdWords will never exceed that amount.
- **It's quick and flexible:** You can set up your account in less than an hour and change your ads, keywords, and budget at any time.
- **You'll know if it works:** You can find out within a short period of time which ads people are clicking on, how many more visits you're getting to your site, and much more.
- **No hidden obligations:** There are no contracts or minimum spend requirements. Once you finish using this free trial voucher, you're under no commitment to

keep going. But, if things are working, you can continue to <u>advertise with AdWords</u> and attract new customers.

1. Set up your AdWords account <u>here</u>.
2. Enter your billing details to activate your account.
3. Enter your voucher code in the Billing Preferences section of your account. This offer is valid only for new AdWords customers.

Voucher Code
****_****_****_****_****

Expiry Date
15th February 2011

For a short step-by-step video on how to create your AdWords account, visit the <u>AdWords Online Classroom</u>.

If you have problems redeeming this coupon, please let us know <u>here</u>.

If you need any assistance setting up, just call **1800 613 820** (Mon –Fri, 9am –5pm) and quote ****_****_****_****_****.

We look forward to welcoming you to Google AdWords.

Yours sincerely,

The AdWords Marketing Team
Google Australia & New Zealand

To help SEM (search engine marketing) businesses offer the right level of service to Google AdWords account holders, Google offers a number of training courses to individuals as part of their SEM accreditation program. The purpose behind this accreditation process is not just to increase the skill levels of SEM professionals, but to increase the number of SEM companies who promote Google AdWords to existing and new customers and ultimately to increase the revenues derived from PPC marketing. This program has been an outstanding success for Google, with hundreds of thousands of individuals around the world developing their skill and expertise while Google's revenues grow twenty percent each year.

Don't get me wrong; this service is an excellent service, and I can assure you if you engage the services of a SEM specialist, you will benefit from increased CTR, reduced CPC costs, and an increase in the volume of traffic to your website. If you take nothing else from this book, then take the recommendation that you need to speak with a SEM specialist.

The logic behind the SEM process and the methodical approach will surprise you in many ways. Their keyword research follows a very similar approach to that outlined in Chapter Two, while the techniques described in Chapter Three (PPC Marketing) will have given you some insight into the approach. While you will see a result from PPC marketing, very quickly, it will take a number of months before the CTR increases and the CPC comes down. Add further delays if your current website does not have a webpage that can be customized as a landing page or the landing page needs to be constructed in the first instance.

To give you some insight into the costs of running a Google AdWords campaign, I want to share with you some statistics from my account. In a twelve-month period ending June 2008, for the keyword phrase "marketing consultants," On the Mark Marketing spent AU$3,270.88 for 2,227 website clicks at an average cost per click of AU$1.47. During this time, our average bid price was AU$2.80.

The keyword phrase was searched a total of 327,894 times, and our ad was ranked on average in position five out of a maximum of ten on page one of Google.

The difference between our bid price of AU$2.80 and the AU$1.47 we paid is testimony to the management of our Google AdWords program, which followed the outline in the previous chapter and Diagram 11. This approach rewarded On the Mark Marketing for delivering a well-ranked landing page with content considered by Google to be highly relevant to the keywords.

A competitor in this same space running an AdWords campaign with poorly constructed ads navigating the visitor to a landing page with content regarded as average and lacking relevancy to the keyword, could have paid a CPC price closer to AU$2.80. Remember also that On the Mark Marketing's average position was five out of ten, so there were four other AdWords advertisers who bid a higher price than our AU$2.80 for those positions.

Google's balancing act between the need for their search engine to offer the most relevant websites and the revenue they derive from AdWords is a struggle. As a result, the door has always been open to enterprising individuals who can find ways to secure the best results for the least cost. Unfortunately, when it comes to AdWords, it's all about who is prepared to pay more for the higher-ranked position. As an example, the CTR and CPC criteria are not part of the equation that guarantees an advertiser one of the top ten positions in AdWords. Google will always award this prize to the company who is willing to spend more with Google for the chosen keyword based on Google's assessment of how frequently that keyword is searched.

Landing pages are critical to the effectiveness of any AdWords campaign, and they need a number of elements working in harmony for the CPC price to be lower than the keyword bid price, and for the CTR to be acceptable. A landing page linked to an AdWords advertisement needs to display sales copy that is a logical extension of the wording contained in the AdWords advertisement that first caught the reader's attention if it is to have any chance of being successful.

There are two types of landing pages, call to action and transactional.

Call to Action

In some situations, we don't want website visitors just coming and going, sometimes we want them to do something on the website that will allow us to engage with them in the future to lead to the sale of a product or service.

Calls to action encourage the website visitors to subscribe, to register, to buy something, to bookmark your website or post. When developing a call to action everything is important: the color of your buttons and supporting elements, the language you use to describe the action, the place on the page where you locate them, the additional elements that encourage people to act. You need to consider all these elements if you are going to get website visitors one-step closer to your objective of making a sale.

Transactional

These landing pages seek to persuade a visitor to complete a transaction, such as filling out a form or interacting with advertisements or other objects on the landing page, with the goal being:

- The immediate or eventual sale of a product or service.
- The collection of customer information for which some offer is extended in exchange for that information.

If information is not provided by the visitor, the page will usually withhold the offer until a pre-determined minimal amount of visitor information has been provided, enough to capture the lead or add the prospect to a mailing list.

The efficiency or quality of the landing page can be measured by its conversion rate, the percentage of visitors who complete the desired action.

The SEM marketers will split all of the keywords into logical groups and run a minimum of two different ads designed for each keyword group. They will also ensure you have a landing page with the right metatag data and page content considered from an SEO perspective to be highly relevant. With all these factors working together, it is likely your SEM program would return high traffic volumes at costs lower than your current CPC price.

If you are running an active Google AdWords account and put all I have outlined into action, then you probably do not need the services of a SEM marketer. If, on the other hand, you have an account but have been paying through the nose, not aware of the options available to you to improve your CTR and CPC pricing, then you may want to consider talking with a SEM marketer.

If you do not have an AdWords account, you should consider trying this option for a couple of reasons. One, you will see instant results from a Google AdWords campaign and two, working in conjunction with the internet strategy in this book, you will see an improved result from the start. Ultimately, you may decide to scale your AdWords campaign back or even suspend it as I have, but it is invaluable experience that will help you understand the importance of keywords.

Chapter Five

SEARCH ENGINE OPTIMIZATION

SEO is growing in market acceptance and is acknowledged as a viable method for securing a page-one ranking on all search engines.

The cost of performing an SEO process on the average website starts at around $5,000 and increases based on the number of pages on your site and the complexity associated with securing a page-one ranking. Once the initial work has been completed, the SEO specialist will charge you a further ten percent of the initial fee every month thereafter to maintain the ranked position. The process is slow, taking between three to six months to achieve a page-one ranking.

After comparing your website to your major competitors, the SEO specialist will perform keyword research to determine what opportunity exists before they recommend a direction to pursue. Changes to sub-domain names, webpage metatags, and website copy follow in an effort to ensure the PageRank of your site delivers the highest rankings possible.

Some companies employ individuals who claim they have the skills to perform these functions, while some may indeed have the skills and are more than capable of delivering a strong SEO result. Unfortunately, the SEO process is constantly changing, so unless the person in your organization is an SEO professional and he or she is in tune with all the changes that are occurring in the SEO market, my recommendation is that you push the process out to an SEO specialist who is working in the SEO space every day.

The best place to start is with the keyword research covered in Chapter Two. Once you have performed this research and reviewed your competitors' websites, you will need to start asking some serious questions about your own website. For example, does your website meet the following essential criteria?

1. Does your website contain all of the keywords from your Chapter Two research?
2. Has your website been constructed so each page has different metatags, including page title, page description, and keywords?
3. Does each page of your website contain text relevant to metatag keywords of that page and your specific product or service offering?
4. Does your webpage copy mention these keywords at least once, but no more than four times?
5. Does your website have different metatags for each webpage?
6. Does your website utilize H1 to H6 page heading tags that incorporate the keywords?
7. Do your website images contain alternative text names that use these keywords?
8. Does your website have any inbound links that incorporate the keywords?
9. Does your website contain hyperlinks that use keywords?
10. Does your website include keywords in the page directory names (for example, is the keyword phrase "internet strategies" included in the page URL<u>www. onthemark.com.au/internet_strategies.htm</u>)?
11. Does your website have a blog?

12. Does your website contain social media links like Facebook, Twitter, etc.?
13. Can your website be found on Google when searching www.yourwebsite.com.au (if not, you have a serious problem).
14. How many listing are shown when you search Google for "www.yourwebsite.com.au" using the "" on either side of the domain name? (The results from this search show how many websites have links to your domain name as well as how many of your pages have been indexed.)
15. Does your website offer access to a regular newsletter?
16. Does your website offer RSS feeds?
17. Does your website offer podcasts and webinars?
18. Have you developed and published articles on the web with links back to your website?

If you have not scored a perfect ten out of ten for the first ten questions, then you have a lot of work to do on your existing website from an SEO perspective. It is important to know the internet strategy outlined in this book will secure for you a page-one ranking on Google within two weeks, independent of the number of points you comply with in the list above, but ticking the boxes on the list will contribute significantly to the overall effectiveness of the internet strategy. For this reason, I encourage you to ensure that as many of the requirements outlined in this section as possible have been met.

The down side of SEO is that Google keeps changing the rules as part of their need to maintain market dominance in the search engine market, and this dominance can only be maintained by ensuring their search engine delivers the most relevant websites to its customers. These changes mean the SEO programs can never be stopped or paused without running the risk of dropping ranked positions.

There are a number of SEO software programs available on the internet, which for a moderate cost will allow you to make the required changes to your website's metatags and page content, many times essential to improving your SEO ranking.

I found the following top nine review at http://seo-software-review.toptenreviews.com and, while I don't want to be drawn into suggesting which product is better, I will say I am a current user of the number three product, iBusiness Promoter.

Diagram 12

To use any of these products effectively, you will need a basic knowledge of HTML programming. I know from my perspective, when I first looked at the HTML code on our website, I found it difficult to understand and even harder to develop code that looked consistently the same over the entire website. While my skills have improved considerably and I now do all of the HTML editing on our website, I still struggle from time to time with some small technical issues.

For those of you who don't know or don't want to know about HTML editing, CSS (cascading style sheets), ASP Net, or Java programming, let me simply say, if you don't have the skills to make changes to your existing website, find a website developer who can help you modify your website onto a CMS (content management system).

Detailed below are nine free CMS applications that will allow you to make instant changes to your website without having to worry about HTML editing or any other website programming language. Changes are made using simple text, which can be created in products like Microsoft Word, copied and pasted into the relevant pages of the CMS-managed webpage. The CMS program converts this text to a stylized format using CSS. Because content is critical as part of the SEO process, the ability to make changes to the copy and meta tags of the various pages on your website, and publishing these changes to your website quickly, is important.

1. **WordPress** is a state-of-the-art publishing platform with a focus on aesthetics, web standards, and usability.

2. **Joomla** is an award-winning content management system (CMS), which enables you to build websites and powerful online applications. Many aspects, including its ease of use and extensibility, have made Joomla one of the most popular website software products available. Best of all, Joomla is an open source solution that is freely available to everyone.

3. **Drupal** is a free software package that allows an individual or a community of users to easily publish, manage, and organize a wide variety of content on a website.

4. **SilverStripe** is a flexible open source content management system that gives everyone involved in a web project the tools they need to do their jobs.

5. **CushyCMS** is a CMS solution that is truly simple to use. It is free for unlimited users, unlimited changes, unlimited pages, and unlimited sites.

6. **Frog** CMS simplifies content management by offering an elegant user interface, flexible templating per page,

simple user management and permissions, as well as the tools necessary for file management.

7. **MODx** helps you take control of your online content. An open source PHP application framework, it frees you to build sites exactly how you want and make them one hundred percent yours. Zero restrictions and fast to build. The solution comes with simple templates in regular HTML/CSS/JS.

8. **TYPOlight** is a web CMS that uses Ajax and Web 2.0 technologies, has a live update feature for those of us who have multiple blogs, gives multi-language support, and hosts a ton of other great features. The fully functional GPL version of dotCMS continues to forge ahead, providing new features and the latest code to a thriving community of developers and users.

9. **ExpressionEngine** is a flexible, feature-rich content management system that empowers thousands of individuals, organizations, and companies around the world to manage their websites.

Chapter Six

UNDERSTANDING GOOGLE'S MARKET DOMINANCE AND HOW THEIR RANKING WORKS

Google is regarded the world over as the top search engine, and it is estimated to hold over sixty-five percent of the global search engine market. The table below shows their market share by country.

Argentina	89.00%	Jan 2008
Australia	87.81%	Jun 2008
Austria	88.00%	Jan 2008
Belgium	96.00%	Mar 2009
Brazil	89.00%	Jan 2008
Bulgaria	80.00%	Dec 2007
Canada	78.00%	Jan 2008
Chile	93.00%	Jan 2008
China	26.60%	Oct 2008
Colombia	91.00%	Jan 2008
Czech Republic	34.50%	Mar 2009
Denmark	92.00%	Jan 2008
Estonia	53.37%	Jul 2008
Finland	92.00%	Jan 2008
France	91.23%	Feb 2009

Germany	93.00%	Mar 2008
Hong Kong	26.00%	Jan 2008
Hungary	96.00%	Aug 2008
Iceland	51.00%	Dec 2007
India	81.40%	Aug 2008
Ireland	76.00%	Jan 2008
Israel	80.00%	2007
Italy	90.00%	Feb 2009
Japan	38.20%	Jan 2009
Korea, South	3.00%	2009
Latvia	97.95%	July 2008
Lithuania	98.18%	Aug 2008
Malaysia	51.00%	Jan 2008
Mexico	88.00%	Jan 2008
Netherlands	95.00%	Dec 2008
New Zealand	72.00%	Jan 2008
Norway	81.00%	Jan 2008
Poland	95.00%	Q4 2008
Portugal	94.00%	Jan 2008
Puerto Rico	57.00%	Jan 2008
Romania	95.21%	Mar 2009
Russia	32.00%	Jan 2008
Singapore	57.00%	Jan 2008
Slovakia	75.60%	Dec 2007
Spain	93.00%	Jan 2008
Sweden	80.00%	Jan 2008
Switzerland	93.00%	Jan 2008
Taiwan	18.00%	Jan 2008
Ukraine	72.42%	Feb 2009
United Kingdom	90.39%	Dec 2008
United States	63.30%	Feb 2009
United States	72.11%	Feb 2009
Venezuela	93.00%	Jan 2008

comScore

Google Sites led the U.S. explicit core search market in August with 65.4 percent market share, followed by Yahoo! Sites with 17.4 percent (up 0.3 percentage points), and Microsoft sites with 11.1 percent (up 0.1 percentage points). Ask Network captured 3.8 percent of explicit core searches, followed by AOL LLC with 2.3 percent.

comScore Explicit Core Search Share Report*
August 2010 vs. July 2010
Total U.S. – Home/Work/University Locations
Source: comScore qSearch

Core Search Entity	Explicit Core Search Share (%)		
	Jul-10	Aug-10	Point Change
Total Explicit Core Search	*100.0%*	*100.0%*	*N/A*
Google Sites	65.8%	65.4%	-0.4
Yahoo! Sites	17.1%	17.4%	0.3
Microsoft Sites	11.0%	11.1%	0.1
Ask Network	3.8%	3.8%	0.0
AOL LLC Network	2.3%	2.3%	0.0

"Explicit Core Search" excludes contextually driven searches that do not reflect specific user intent to interact with the search results.

Nearly 15.7 billion explicit core searches were conducted in August. Google Sites ranked first with 10.3 billion searches, followed by Yahoo! Sites in second with 2.7 billion (up 3 percent) and Microsoft Sites in third with 1.7 billion (up 2 percent). Ask Network accounted for 598 million explicit core searches (up 2 percent), followed by AOL LLC Network with 366 million.

comScore Explicit Core Search Query Report
August 2010 vs. July 2010
Total U.S. – Home/Work/University Locations
Source: comScore qSearch

Core Search Entity	Explicit Core Search Queries (MM)		
	Jul-10	**Aug-10**	**Percent Change**
Total Explicit Core Search	15,589	15,695	1%
Google Sites	10,263	10,259	0%
Yahoo! Sites	2,661	2,728	3%
Microsoft Sites	1,712	1,744	2%
Ask Network	588	598	2%
AOL LLC Network	365	366	0%

U.S. Total Core Search

Google Sites accounted for 60.5 percent of total core search queries conducted, followed by Yahoo! Sites with 21.0 percent and Microsoft Sites with 12.8 percent. Ask Network captured 3.5 percent of total search queries, followed by AOL LLC with 2.2 percent.

comScore Total Core Search Share Report*
August 2010 vs. July 2010
Total U.S. – Home/Work/University Locations
Source: comScore qSearch

Core Search Entity	Total Core Search Share (%)		
	Jul-10	**Aug-10**	**Point Change**
Total Core Search	100.0%	100.0%	N/A
Google Sites	61.6%	60.5%	-1.1

Yahoo! Sites	20.1%	21.0%	0.9
Microsoft Sites	12.6%	12.8%	0.2
Ask Network	3.5%	3.5%	0.0
AOL LLC Network	2.2%	2.2%	0.0

* "Total Core Search" is based on the five major search engines, includingpartner searches, cross-channel searches, and contextual searches. Searchesfor mapping, local directory, and user-generated video sites that are not on thecore domain of the five search engines are not included in these numbers.

Americans conducted more than 16.9 billion total core search queries in August with Google Sites leading with 10.3 billion searches, followed by Yahoo! Sites with 3.6 billion and Microsoft Sites with 2.2 billion.

comScore Total Core Search Query Report
August 2010 vs. July 2010
Total U.S. – Home/Work/University Locations
Source: comScore qSearch

Core Search Entity	Total Core Search Queries (MM)		
	Jul-10	**Aug-10**	**Percent Change**
Total Core Search	16,673	16,950	2%
Google Sites	10,263	10,259	0%
Yahoo! Sites	3,351	3,562	6%
Microsoft Sites	2,106	2,166	3%
Ask Network	588	598	2%
AOL LLC Network	365	366	0%

A Note about September 2010 qSearch Reporting

comScore's ability to report qSearch data for September 2010 will not be impacted by recent changes in the search landscape, including the introduction of Google Instant Search and Microsoft's powering of specific channels of search activity within Yahoo! Google's introduction of Instant Search does not disrupt comScore's ability to measure search activity consistently, but does introduce a new dynamic that will be addressed in our data-collection methodology.

The Google website is one of the three most visited websites, with over 10.2 billion searches conducted in the USA alone in July 2010. It has localized websites for over 150 countries, operating in 117 different languages, and is supported by a server farm estimated at over 100,000 servers.

Google commenced operations in 1996 at Stanford University, when both founding partners were students. They received start-up venture capital of $100,000 in 1998, and in 1999 they received $25 million in venture capital. Their reported revenue in 2009 was 23.6 billion dollars, of which over 99 percent is derived from their paid advertising program AdWords

Google's innovations in search engine technology made them number one in the marketplace, but interestingly, they did not make a profit until they started auctioning keywords with AdWords advertisements appearing alongside the search results. Research shows that Google's auction methodology, invented internally and so important to its success, is far more innovative than auction experts once believed.

The other search engines are only now matching some of Google's innovations. For instance, Yahoo! gives the top spot on its search results page to the advertiser who pays the most per click, while Google gives its best position to the advertiser who is likely to pay Google the most in total. This assessment is based on the PPC multiplied by Google's estimate of the likelihood that someone will actually click on the ad.

What makes Google's keyword auction so different is the price you bid to win the auction is often higher than the price you actually pay.

PageRank is a probability distribution used to represent the likelihood that a person randomly clicking on links will arrive at any particular page. The PageRank computations require several passes, called "iterations," through the collection to adjust approximate PageRank values to more accurately reflect the theoretical true value.

A probability is expressed as a numeric value between 0 and 1, with 0.5 probability being expressed as a "50 percent chance" of something happening. Hence, a PageRank of 0.5 means there is a 50 percent chance that a person clicking on a random link will be directed to the webpage with the 0.5 PageRank.

Simplified Algorithm

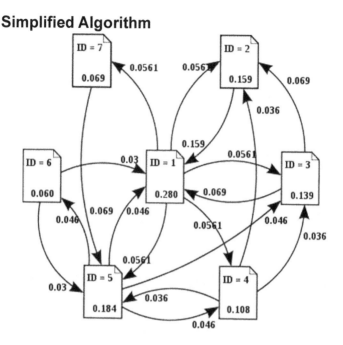

How PageRank Works

Assume a small universe of four webpages: **A**, **B**, **C,** and **D**. The initial approximation of PageRank would be evenly divided between these four webpages. Hence, each webpage would begin with an estimated PageRank of 0.25.

In the original form of PageRank, initial values were simply 1. This meant that the sum of all pages was the total number of pages on the web. Later versions of PageRank (see the formulas below) would assume a probability distribution between 0 and 1. Here, a simple probability distribution will be used—hence the initial value of 0.25.

If webpages **B**, **C**, and **D** each only link to **A**, they would each confer 0.25 PageRank to **A**. All PageRank **PR** in this simplistic system would thus gather to **A** because all links would be pointing to **A**, resulting in a PageRank of 0.75.

$$PR(A) = PR(B) + PR(C) + PR(D).$$

Suppose that page **B** has a link to page **C** as well as to page **A**, while page **D** has links to all three pages. The *value of the link-votes is divided among all the outbound links on a page*. Thus, page **B** gives a vote worth 0.125 to page **A** and a vote worth 0.125 to page **C**. Only one third of **D**'s PageRank is counted for **A**'s PageRank (approximately 0.083).

$$PR(A) = \frac{PR(B)}{2} + \frac{PR(C)}{1} + \frac{PR(D)}{3}$$

In other words, the PageRank conferred by an outbound link is equal to the webpage's own PageRank score divided by the normalized number of outbound links **L( )** (it is assumed that links to specific URLs only count once per webpage).

$$PR(A) = \frac{PR(B)}{L(B)} + \frac{PR(C)}{L(C)} + \frac{PR(D)}{L(D)}$$

In the general case, the PageRank value for any page **u** can be expressed as:

$$PR(u) = \sum_{v \in Bu} + \frac{PR(v)}{L(v)} \ ,$$

The PageRank value for a page **u** is dependent on the PageRank values for each page **v** out of the set **B$_u$** (this set contains all pages linking to page **u**), divided by the number **L(v)** of links from page **v**.

Damping Factor

The PageRank theory holds that even an imaginary surfer who is randomly clicking on links will eventually stop clicking. The probability, at any step, that the person will continue is a damping factor *d*. Various studies have tested different damping factors, but it is generally assumed that the damping factor will be set around 0.85.

The damping factor is subtracted from 1 (and in some variations of the algorithm, the result is divided by the number of webpages (N) in the collection), and this term is then added to the product of the damping factor and the sum of the incoming PageRank scores. That is,

$$PR(A) = \left(\frac{PR(B)}{L(B)} + \frac{PR(C)}{L(C)} + \frac{PR(D)}{L(D)} + \ldots \right)$$

So, any page's PageRank is derived, in large part, from the PageRanks of other pages. The damping factor adjusts the derived value downward. The original paper, however, gave the following formula, which has led to some confusion:

$$PR(A) = 1 - d + d \left(\frac{PR(B)}{L(B)} + \frac{PR(C)}{L(C)} + \frac{PR(D)}{L(D)} + \ldots \right)$$

The difference between them is that the PageRank values in the first formula sum to one, while in the second formula each PageRank gets multiplied by *N* and the sum becomes *N*.

To be more specific, in the latter formula, the probability for the random surfer reaching a page is weighted by the total number of webpages. So, in this version, PageRank is an expected value for the random surfer visiting a page, when he restarts this procedure as often as the web has pages. If the web had 100 pages and a page had a PageRank value of 2, the random surfer would reach that page in an average twice if he restarts 100 times. Basically, the two formulas do not differ fundamentally from each other. A PageRank that has been calculated by using the former formula has to be multiplied by the total number of webpages to get the according PageRank that would have been calculated by using the latter formula.

Google recalculates PageRank scores each time it crawls the Web and rebuilds its index. As Google increases the number of documents in its collection, the initial approximation of PageRank decreases for all webpages.

The formula uses a model of a random surfer who gets bored after several clicks and switches to a random page. The PageRank value of a page reflects the chance that the random surfer will land on that page by clicking on a link. It can be understood as a Markov chain in which the states are pages, and the transitions are all equally probable, and are the links between pages.

If a page has no links to other pages, it becomes a sink, and therefore terminates the random surfing process. If the random surfer arrives at a sink page, it picks another URL at random and continues surfing again.

When calculating PageRank, pages with no outbound links are assumed to link out to all other pages in the collection. Their PageRank scores are therefore divided evenly among all other pages from that website. In other words, to be fair with pages that are not sinks, these random transitions are added to all nodes in the web, with a residual probability of usually $d = 0.85$, estimated from the frequency that an average surfer uses his or her browser's bookmark feature.

So, the equation is as follows:

$$PR(pi) = \frac{1 - d}{N} + d \sum_{pj \in M(pi)} \frac{PR(pj)}{L(pj)}$$

Where p_1, p_2, p_N are the pages under consideration, $M(p_i)$ is the set of pages that link to p_i, $L(p_j)$ is the number of outbound links on page p_j, and N is the total number of pages.

The PageRank values are the entries of the dominant eigenvector of the modified adjacency matrix. This makes PageRank a particularly elegant metric: the eigenvector is

$$R = \begin{bmatrix} PR\ (p1) \\ PR\ (p2) \\ \vdots \\ PR\ (pN) \end{bmatrix}$$

where **R** is the solution of the equation

$$R = \begin{bmatrix} d)\ /N \\ (1 - d)\ /N \\ \cdot \\ \cdot \\ (1 - d)\ /N \end{bmatrix} + d \begin{bmatrix} \ell(P1,P1) & \ell(P2,p2) & \dots & \ell(P1,PN) \\ \ell(P2,P1) & & & \\ & \ddots & \ell(Pi,Pj) & \vdots \\ \ell(PN,P1) & \dots & & \ell(PN,PN) \end{bmatrix} R$$

Where the adjacency function $e(Pi, Pj)$ is 0 if page Pj_j does not link to p_i, and normalized such that, for each j

$$\sum_{i=1}^{N} l(Pi \, , \, Pj) = 1$$
,

The elements of each column sum up to 1, so the matrix is a stochastic matrix (for more details, see the computation section below). Thus, this is a variant of the eigenvector centrality measure used commonly in network analysis.

Because of the large eigengap of the modified adjacency matrix above, the values of the PageRank eigenvector are fast to approximate (only a few iterations are needed).

As a result of Markov theory, it can be shown that the PageRank of a page is the probability of being at that page after lots of clicks. This happens to equal t^{-1} where t is the expectation of the number of clicks (or random jumps) required to get from the page back to itself.

The main disadvantage is that it favors older pages, because a new page, even a very good one, will not have many links unless it is part of an existing site (a site being a densely connected set of pages, such as Wikipedia). The Google Directory (itself a derivative of the Open Directory Project) allows users to see results sorted by PageRank within categories.

The Google Directory is the only service offered by Google where PageRank directly determines display order. In Google's other search services (such as its primary Web search), PageRank is used to weight the relevance scores of pages shown in search results.

Google is known to penalize link farms and other schemes designed to artificially inflate PageRank. In December 2007,

Google started *actively* penalizing sites selling paid text links. How Google identifies link farms and other PageRank manipulation tools are among Google's trade secrets.

Computation

To summarize, PageRank can be either computed iteratively or algebraically. The iterative method can be viewed differently as the power iteration method, or power method. The basic mathematical operations performed in the iterative method and the power method are identical.

Iterative

In the former case, at **t = 0**, an initial probability distribution is assumed, usually

$$PR\ (pi\ ;\ 0)\ =\ \frac{1}{N.}$$

At each time step, the computation, as detailed above, yields

$$PR(pi;\ t + 1) = \frac{1 - d}{N} + d \sum_{pj \in M(pi)} \frac{PR(pj\ ;\ t)}{L(pj)}$$

or in matrix notation

$$R\ (t + 1) = dMR(t) + \frac{1 - d}{N}\ 1$$

Where **R**$i(t)$ = $PR(pi;\ t)$ and **1** is the column vector of length N containing only ones.

The matrix **M** is defined as

$$Mij = \left\{ \begin{array}{cc} 1/L(pj), & \text{if } j \text{ links to } i \\ 0, & \text{otherwise} \end{array} \right.$$

i.e., $M := (K^{-1} A)^{T}$

Where A denotes the adjacency matrix of the graph and K is the diagonal matrix with the outdegrees in the diagonal.

The computation ends when for some small ε

$$\left| R(t+1) - R(t) \right| < \epsilon$$

i.e., when convergence is assumed.

Algebraic

In the latter case, for $T \rightarrow \infty$ (i.e., in the steady state), the above equation (*) reads

$$R = dMR + \frac{1-d}{N} 1 \quad (**)$$

The solution is given by

$$R = (I - dM)^{-1} \frac{1-d}{N} 1$$

with the identity matrix $\mathbf{I}$.

The solution exists and is unique for $0 < d < 1$. This can be seen by noting that M is by construction a stochastic matrix and hence has an eigenvalue equal to one because of the Perron-Frobenius theorem.

Power Method

If the matrix $\mathbf{M}$ is a transition probability, i.e., column-stochastic with no columns consisting of just zeros and $\mathbf{R}$ is a probability distribution (i.e., $\mathbf{R} = 1$, $\mathbf{ER} = 1$ where $\mathbf{E}$ is matrix of all ones), Eq. (**) is equivalent to

$$R = \left(dM + \frac{1-d}{N} E\right) R =: \ \widehat{\mathcal{M}} R$$

Hence, PageRank R is the principal eigenvector of $\widehat{\mathcal{M}}$. A fast and easy way to compute this is using the power method: starting with an arbitrary vector $x(0)$, the operator $\mathbf{M}$ is applied in succession, i.e.,

$$x(t+1) = \widehat{\mathcal{M}} x(t)$$

until

$$x(t+1) - x(t) \,|\, < \varepsilon.$$

Note that in Eq. (***) the matrix on the right-hand side in the parenthesis can be interpreted as

$$\frac{1-d}{N} I = (1-d) P 1^t$$

where $\mathbf{P}$ is an initial probability distribution. In the current case

$$P := \frac{1}{N} 1$$

Finally, if M has columns with only zero values, they should be replaced with the initial probability vector **P**. In other words,

$$M' := M = D$$

where the matrix D is defined as

$$D := DP^t$$

with

$$\mathbf{D}i = \begin{cases} 1 & \text{if } L\ (pi) = 0 \\ 0, & \text{otherwise} \end{cases}$$

In this case, the above two computations using M only give the same PageRank if their results are normalized:

$$\mathbf{R}\ \text{power} = \frac{\mathbf{R}\ \text{iterative}}{|\ \mathbf{R}\ \text{iterative}\ |} = \frac{\mathbf{R}\ \text{algebraic}}{|\ \mathbf{R}\ \text{algebraic}\ |}$$

Efficiency

Depending on the framework used to perform the computation, the exact implementation of the methods, and the required accuracy of the result, the computation time of these methods can vary greatly.

Google Toolbar

The Google Toolbar's PageRank feature displays a visited page's PageRank as a whole number between 0 and 10. The most popular websites have a PageRank of 10. The least have a PageRank of 0. Google has not disclosed the precise method for determining a Toolbar PageRank value. The displayed value is not the actual value Google uses, so it is only a rough guide. Toolbar PageRank is different from Google PageRank because the PageRank displayed in the toolbar is not 100 percent reflective of the way Google judges the value of a website.

The PageRank of a particular page is roughly based upon the quantity of inbound links as well as the PageRank of the pages providing the links. Other factors are also part of the algorithm, such as the size of a page, the number of changes and its up-to-datedness, the key texts in headlines, and the words of hyperlinked anchor texts.

The Google Toolbar's PageRank is updated two times a year, so often shows out-of-date values.

SERP Rank

The search engine results page (SERP) is the actual result returned by a search engine in response to a keyword query. The SERP consists of a list of links to webpages with associated text snippets. The SERP rank of a webpage refers to the placement of the corresponding link on the SERP, where higher placement means higher SERP rank. The SERP rank of a webpage is not only a function of its PageRank, but depends on a relatively large and continuously adjusted set of factors (over 200), commonly referred to by internet marketers as "Google Love." Search engine optimization (SEO) is aimed at achieving the highest possible SERP rank for a website or a set of webpages.

With the introduction of Google Places into the mainstream organic SERP, PageRank plays little to no role in ranking a business in the local business results. While the theory of citations is still computed in their algorithm, PageRank is not a factor, since Google ranks business listings and not webpages.

Google Directory PageRank

The Google Directory PageRank is an eight-unit measurement. These values can be viewed in the Google Directory. Unlike the Google Toolbar, which shows the PageRank value by a mouse over of the green bar, the Google Directory does not show the PageRank as a numeric value, but only as a green bar.

False or Spoofed PageRank

While the PageRank shown in the toolbar is considered to be derived from an accurate PageRank value (at some time prior to the time of publication by Google) for most sites, it must be noted that this value was at one time easily manipulated. A previous flaw was that any low PageRank page that was redirected via an HTTP 302 response or a "refresh" metatag to a high PageRank page caused the lower PageRank page to acquire the PageRank of the destination page. In theory, a new PR0 page with no incoming links could have been redirected to the Google home page, which is a PR10, and then the PR of the new page would be upgraded to a PR10. This spoofing technique, also known as 302 Google jacking, was a known failing or bug in the system. Any page's PageRank could have been spoofed to a higher or lower number of the webmaster's choice, and only Google had access to the real PageRank of the page. Spoofing is generally detected by running a Google search for a URL with questionable PageRank, as the results will display the URL of an entirely different site (the one redirected to) in its results.

Manipulating PageRank

For search engine optimization purposes, some companies offer to sell high PageRank links to webmasters. As links from higher-PR pages are believed to be more valuable, they tend to be more expensive. It can be an effective and viable marketing strategy to buy link advertisements on content pages of quality and relevant sites to drive traffic and increase a webmaster's link popularity. However, Google has publicly warned webmasters that if they are or were discovered to be selling links for the purpose of conferring PageRank and reputation, their links would be devalued (ignored in the calculation of other pages' PageRanks). The practice of buying and selling links is intensely debated across the webmaster community. Google advises webmasters to use the nofollow HTML attribute value on sponsored links.

The Intentional Surfer Model

The original PageRank algorithm reflects the so-called random surfer model, meaning that the PageRank of a particular page is derived from the theoretical probability of visiting that page when clicking on links at random. However, real users do not randomly surf the web, but follow links according to their interests and intention. A page-ranking model that reflects the importance of a particular page as a function of how many actual visits it receives by real users is called the intentional surfer model.

The Google Toolbar sends information to Google for every page visited, and thereby provides a basis for computing PageRank based on the intentional surfer model. The introduction of the nofollow attribute by Google to combat spamdexing has the side effect that webmasters commonly use it on outgoing links to increase their own PageRank. This causes a loss of actual links for the web crawlers to follow, thereby making the original PageRank algorithm based on the random surfer model potentially unreliable. Using information about users' browsing habits provided by the Google Toolbar partly compensates for the loss of information caused by the nofollow attribute. The SERP rank of a page, which determines a page's actual placement in the search results, is based on a combination of the random surfer model (PageRank) and the intentional surfer model (browsing habits), in addition to other factors.

Other Uses

A version of PageRank has recently been proposed as a replacement for the traditional Institute for Scientific Information (ISI) impact factor and implemented at eigenfactor.org. Instead of merely counting total citations to a journal, the "importance" of each citation is determined in a PageRank fashion.

A similar new use of PageRank is to rank academic doctoral programs based on their records of placing their graduates in faculty positions. In PageRank terms, academic departments link to each other by hiring their faculty from each other (and from themselves).

PageRank has been used to rank spaces or streets to predict how many people (pedestrians or vehicles) come to the individual spaces or streets. In lexical semantics, it has been used to perform word sense disambiguation and to automatically rank WordNet synsets according to how strongly they possess a given semantic property, such as positivity or negativity.

A dynamic weighting method similar to PageRank has been used to generate customized reading lists based on the link structure of Wikipedia.

A web crawler may use PageRank as one of a number of importance metrics it uses to determine which URL to visit during a crawl of the web. One of the early working papers that was used in the creation of Google is efficient crawling through URL ordering, which discusses the use of a number of different importance metrics to determine how deeply and how much of a site Google will crawl. PageRank is presented as one of a number of these importance metrics, though there are others listed, such as the number of inbound and outbound links for a URL and the distance from the root directory on a site to the URL.

The PageRank may also be used as a methodology to measure the apparent impact of a community like the blogosphere on the overall web itself. This approach therefore uses the PageRank to measure the distribution of attention in reflection of the scale-free network paradigm.

In any ecosystem, a modified version of PageRank may be used to determine species that are essential to the continuing health of the environment.

Google's `rel="nofollow"` **Option**

In early 2005, Google implemented a new value, "nofollow," for the rel attribute of HTML link and anchor elements, so that website developers and bloggers could make links that Google will not consider for the purposes of PageRank—they are links that no longer constitute a "vote" in the PageRank system. The nofollow relationship was added in an attempt to help combat spamdexing.

As an example, people could previously create many message-board posts with links to their website to artificially inflate their PageRank. With the nofollow value, message-board administrators can modify their code to automatically insert rel="nofollow" to all hyperlinks in posts, thus preventing PageRank from being affected by those particular posts. This method of avoidance, however, has various drawbacks, such as reducing the link value of legitimate comments.

In an effort to manually control the flow of PageRank among pages within a website, many webmasters practice what is known as PageRank sculpting, which is the act of strategically placing the nofollow attribute on certain internal links of a website in order to funnel PageRank towards those pages the webmaster deemed most important. This tactic has been used since the inception of the nofollow attribute, but the technique has been thought by many to have lost its effectiveness.

The PageRank algebra and content in this section of the book was taken from Wikipedia and is one of the few published examples of how PageRank works.

Chapter Seven

SO YOU WANT A GOOGLE PAGE-ONE RANKING?

Every day my e-mail inbox contains a number of e-mails offering to secure for me a page-one ranking. On average, this equates to 3.8 e-mails every business day, totaling over 1,000 e-mails every year. They all guarantee to secure a page-one ranking for me, but what they don't tell me is how long the process will take, how much it's going to cost, or how specifically they intend to fulfill their guarantee.

Most of the e-mail addresses these e-mails are sent to have been illegally collected from websites using e-mail list-building software designed to collect information for developing a database. Most of them are spam and are just plain rubbish; some, after investigation, appear to know what they are talking about, while a few are condescending enough to tell me they like my website, acknowledge it's well ranked, but go on to tell me the same old stuff: "our approach to SEO will guarantee you a page-one ranking."

Assuming you don't have the skills associated with performing an SEO function on your website, you will be faced with the difficult task of finding someone who can. I dare say you will probably go to Google and search for the term SEO or for search engine optimization, be presented with a list, navigate through several websites, and, based on what you now know, select a partner and move forward.

Having read the previous chapters and hopefully having a better understanding of the work that needs to be performed, you may want to read the balance of this chapter and then discover the strategy that will change the SEO market forever.

Perhaps the best source of information when considering traditional approaches to securing a page-one ranking is Google itself. Detailed below is a selection of some of the guidelines provided by Google to website developers.

Design and Content Guidelines

- Make a site with a clear hierarchy and text links. Every page should be reachable from at least one static text link.

- Offer a site map to your users with links that point to the important parts of your site. If the site map has an extremely large number of links, you may want to break the site map into multiple pages.

- Keep the links on a given page to a reasonable number.

- Create a useful, information-rich site, and write pages that clearly and accurately describe your content.

- Think about the words users would type to find your pages, and make sure that your site actually includes those words within it.

- Try to use text instead of images to display important names, content, or links. The Google crawler does not recognize text contained in images. If you must use images for textual content, consider using the "ALT" attribute to include a few words of descriptive text.

- Make sure that your <title> elements and ALT attributes are descriptive and accurate.

- Check for broken links and correct HTML.
- If you decide to use dynamic pages (i.e. the URL contains a "?" character), be aware that not every search engine spider crawls dynamic pages as well as static pages. It helps to keep the parameters short and the number of them few.
- Review our image guidelines for best practices on publishing images.

Technical Guidelines

- Use a text browser, such as Lynx, to examine your site because most search engine spiders see your site much as Lynx would. If fancy features such as JavaScript, cookies, session IDs, frames, DHTML, or Flash keep you from seeing your entire website in a text browser, then search engine spiders may have trouble crawling your site.
- Allow search bots to crawl your sites without session IDs or arguments that track their path through the site. These techniques are useful for tracking individual user behavior, but the access pattern of bots is entirely different. Using these techniques may result in incomplete indexing of your site, as bots may not be able to eliminate URLs that look different but actually point to the same page.
- Make sure your web server supports the If-Modified-Since HTTP header. This feature allows your web server to tell Google whether your content has changed since they last crawled your site. Supporting this feature saves you bandwidth and overhead.
- Make use of the robots.txt file on your web server. This file tells crawlers which directories can or cannot be

crawled. Make sure it's current for your site so that you don't accidentally block the Googlebot crawler. Visit http://www.robotstxt.org/faq.html to learn how to instruct robots when they visit your site. You can test your robots.txt file to make sure you're using it correctly with the robots.txt analysis tool available in Google Webmaster Tools.

- Make reasonable efforts to ensure that advertisements do not affect search engine rankings. For example, Google's AdSense ads and DoubleClick links are blocked from being crawled by a robots.txt file.

- If your company buys a content management system, make sure that the system creates pages and links that search engines can crawl.

- Use robots.txt to prevent crawling of search results pages or other auto-generated pages that don't add much value for users coming from search engines.

- Test your site to make sure that it appears correctly in different browsers.

- Monitor your site's performance and optimize load times. Google's goal is to provide users with the most relevant results and a great user experience. Fast sites increase user satisfaction and improve the overall quality of the web (especially for those users with slow internet connections), and Google's desire is for webmasters to improve their sites so the overall speed of the web improves.

- Google strongly recommends that all webmasters regularly monitor site performance using Page Speed, YSlow, WebPagetest, or other tools. For more information, tools, and resources, see Let's Make The Web Faster. In addition, the Site Performance tool in

Webmaster Tools shows the speed of your website as experienced by users around the world.

Quality Guidelines

These quality guidelines cover the most common forms of deceptive or manipulative behavior, but Google may respond negatively to other misleading practices not listed here (e.g. tricking users by registering misspellings of well-known websites). It's not safe to assume that just because a specific deceptive technique isn't included on this page, Google approves of it. Webmasters who spend their energies upholding the spirit of the basic principles will provide a much better user experience and subsequently enjoy better ranking than those who spend their time looking for loopholes they can exploit.

If you believe that another site is abusing Google's quality guidelines, please report that site at https://www.google.com/webmasters/tools/spamreport. Google prefers developing scalable and automated solutions to problems, so they attempt to minimize hand-to-hand spam fighting. The spam reports Google receives are used to create scalable algorithms that recognize and block future spam attempts.

Quality Guidelines—Basic Principles

- Make pages primarily for users, not for search engines. Don't deceive your users or present different content to search engines than you display to users, which is commonly referred to as "cloaking."
- Avoid tricks intended to improve search engine rankings. A good rule of thumb is whether you'd feel comfortable explaining what you've done to a website that competes with you. Another useful test is to ask, "Does this help my users? Would I do this if search engines didn't exist?"

- Don't participate in link schemes designed to increase your site's ranking or PageRank. In particular, avoid links to web spammers or "bad neighborhoods" on the web, as your own ranking may be affected adversely by those links.

- Don't use unauthorized computer programs to submit pages, check rankings, etc. Such programs consume computing resources and violate Google's Terms of Service. Google does not recommend the use of products such as WebPosition Gold™ that send automatic or programmatic queries to Google.

Quality Guidelines—Specific Guidelines

- Avoid hidden text or hidden links.
- Don't use cloaking or sneaky redirects.
- Don't send automated queries to Google.
- Don't load pages with irrelevant keywords.
- Don't create multiple pages, subdomains, or domains with duplicate content.
- Don't create pages with malicious behavior, such as phishing or installing viruses, trojans, or other badware.
- Avoid "doorway" pages created just for search engines or other "cookie cutter" approaches such as affiliate programs with little or no original content.
- If your site participates in an affiliate program, make sure that your site adds value. Provide unique and relevant content that gives users a reason to visit your site first.

Yahoo! and Bing also offer their own set of instructions, but they are nowhere near as comprehensive as Google's.

Clearly, there is a lot of work in securing a page-one ranking as well as maintain that ranking on a go-forward basis. The point that needs to be made here is that you don't need to do all this work to secure the ranking. Instead, you can follow the guidelines in the next chapter, secure a page-one ranking within two weeks, and hold that position forever.

It isn't necessary to perform all of the other functions outlined in the book, however, ensuring you are compliant with these requirements will provide you with multiple page-one rankings. Holding two or even three out of the top ten positions simply increases your chances of winning business while pushing the competition onto page two. Once relegated to page two, the only options available are to increase their SEO ranking and replace one of the other competitors on page one or increase their PPC price with Google AdWords in order to achieve a higher ranking in the sponsored section. The problem with this action is that to stay high on the sponsored section they will need to be prepared to outbid their competition to stay there.

The additional costs associated with either the SEO or Google AdWords options will erode the competitor's profitability while the saving you have generated could be directed into other marketing activities designed to grow sales, strengthening your market positioning or brand marketing.

Chapter Eight

INTERNET STRATEGIES: THE REVOLUTION IN PAGE-ONE RANKINGS CONCEPT

While I was working on a client's SEO ranking last year, I had an epiphany. It struck me the current methodology used by all SEO service providers was not capable of sustaining long-term, page-one SEO rankings.

The basis for this opinion is simple; at the same time I was performing an SEO function for my client, it was likely that another SEO agents was doing the same thing for one of my client's competitors. The results of this battle between SEO experts could ultimately see only one "number-one-ranked position winner" and an ongoing battle to maintain the ranking.

Assuming you read this book from the front and didn't just jump to this chapter to find out the answer, you should have a good understanding of the processes associated with developing website traffic and how to achieve an SEO page-one ranking. I would, however, encourage you to go back and read the earlier chapters when you get a chance, as they will influence the outcomes from a long-term strategy perspective.

To achieve a page-one SEO ranking requires the adoption of several strategies and a number of actions as well as the ongoing need to maintain this work if you want to remain number one on page one of any search engine.

A key part of this process is the selection of keywords your target audience will use to find a website on the internet that offers the product or service they want to purchase. Blending these keywords into the website metadata, page content, links, hyperlinks, alternative image file names, and anything else that matters will go a long way to securing the result you need, but the problem is your competitor is doing the same thing with possibly the same keywords.

So let's go back to the beginning, to the selection of the domain name that your website is hosted under; from my perspective, that domain name was www.onthemark.com.au. The services that I wanted On the Mark Marketing to promote and sell were things like marketing consultants, branding strategies, internet strategies, sales strategies, search engine optimization, and rapid business builder.

I was curious to know how frequently these keywords were searched on Google, so given I already had a Google AdWords account, and knowing this facility was available to users, I logged onto my account and ran a keyword search. I was able to download an Excel CSV file listing keywords along with the frequency with which each of the keywords was searched regionally and internationally and how much the PPC was for each keyword. While Google uses this tool to convince you to extend the number of keywords in your AdWords campaign, it is a good source of valuable information and it's free to anyone with a Google account. The ability to see how people use search engines and what they search for is the starting point to understanding how they think and what they are looking for.

I sorted the Excel file by local search volumes, highest to lowest, and selected several keywords with the highest search frequency. I then opened an Explorer window and started to enter the keywords into Google. As I typed the keywords, Google's drop down window extended, offering me confirmation of all the keyword searches. This is a recent innovation on the part of Google to make it easier for the user to navigate their website.

Armed with this newfound information, I opened the website of a local domain name provider and started to search for domain names that contained the keyword phrase from the Excel spreadsheet. To my surprise, almost all of the high-volume keywords were available to purchase as domain names. I registered each of the key domain names, along with thirty or so variations, and started the process that would secure me several page-one rankings on Google.

To test the effectiveness of the strategy, I created a one-page clone of www.onthemark.com.au called www.marketingconsultantssydney.com.au, changing all of the internal links to open a new browser session on the respective pages on the www.onthemark.com.au website. I also set up a 301 redirection to www.onthemark.com.au from the domain name www.rapidbusinessbuilder.com.au.

I then logged both domain names with the search engines outlined in Chapter One. A few days later, I was able to confirm the domain names had been crawled by Google and, to my surprise, three days later the websites for this domain name were sitting on page one of Google.

Based on these results, I approached a couple of my existing clients and offered them the opportunity to test this strategy. Applying the same rules and procedures, I was able to purchase several domain names for each client and to generate page-one rankings for them in the same time period as I was able to with my own domain names.

What was interesting from On the Mark's perspective was when I searched the keyword phrase "rapid business builders;" I found the first two listings were both my websites, as shown in Diagram 13.

Diagram 13

When I changed the location on the left-hand column of Google to "pages from Australia," the situation was even better, with the first three listings all being owned by On the Mark Marketing, as shown in Diagram 14.

Diagram 14

Having the first three listing on page one of Google for the search term "rapid business builders" has to increase my chances of winning business. My total cost for this page-one ranking was $12.00 a year for the domain name, $46.00 for hosting the second website, $30.00 for a 301 redirection from a third domain name, and a handful of hours to massage the content of a one-page clone of the www.onthemark.com.au website.

Had I used traditional SEO techniques, it would have cost an initial investment of $5,000 and a further $500 each month for as long as I wanted to maintain that page-one ranking. Remember, that if any of my competitors were doing the same thing, I was only going to maintain my advantage by the continual refinement and changes to the SEO values, sometimes maintaining and sometimes dropping in my ranked position.

Following are some examples of the work I have done for On the Mark Marketing and two other clients.

On the Mark Marketing Pty Ltd

To identify the extent of the page-one rankings for all the keywords on the following domain names, I ran a search engine ranking report.

www.onthemark.com.au
www.onthemarkmarketing.com.au
www.marketingconsultants.com.au
www.rapidbusinessbuilders.com.au

The report shows a total of forty (40) top-ten, page-one rankings for the nine (9) keywords on these websites (see Diagram 15).

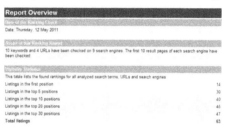

Report Overview	
Date of the Ranking Check	
Date: Thursday, 12 May 2011	
Scope of the Ranking Report	
10 keywords and 4 URLs have been checked on 9 search engines. The first 10 result pages of each search engine have been checked.	
Visibility Statistics	
This table lists the found rankings for all analyzed search terms, URLs and search engines	
Listings in the first position	14
Listings in the top 5 positions	30
Listings in the top 10 positions	40
Listings in the top 20 positions	46
Listings in the top 30 positions	47
Total listings	63

Diagram 15

Topstuff 4 Business Pty Ltd

To identify the extent of the page-one rankings for all the keywords on the following domain names, I ran a search engine ranking report for Topstuff.

www.business-communications.com.au
www.businessmobiledeals.com.au
www.businessmobilephonedeals.com.au
www.business-mobile-phones.com.au
www.business-mobiles.com.au
www.mobilephonebusiness.com.au

The report showed a total of thirty-six (36) top-ten, page-one rankings for the ten (10) keywords on these websites (see Diagram 16 B).

What is interesting with this example is the client's website http://www.businessmobiledeals.com.au is ranked ahead of Telstra, Optus, and Vodafone - the three largest Telco's operating in Australia (see Diagram 16 A).

Diagram 16 A

Report Overview	
Date of the Ranking Check	
Date: Friday, 25 March 2011	
Detail of this Ranking Report	
10 keywords and 6 URLs have been checked on 9 search engines. The first 10 result pages of each search engine have been checked	
Visibility Statistics	
This table lists the found rankings for all analyzed search terms, URLs and search engines	
Listings in the first position	16
Listings in the top 5 positions	23
Listings in the top 10 positions	36
Listings in the top 20 positions	44
Listings in the top 30 positions	54
Total listings	78

Diagram 16 B

Unfortunately, as I was finishing the book, Topstuff 4 Business stopped trading as a Vodafone dealer due to significant network performance issues being experienced by Vodafone. The situation was further complicated when Vodafone's network security was breached, allowing the confidential details of a significant number of their customers to be accessed by hackers.

It was reported in the *Sydney Morning Herald* on May 5, 2011 that Vodafone was losing over 100,000 customers a month. The significant financial implication associated with this situation forced Topstuff 4 Business to make the decision to exit the mobile telecommunications market in Australia.

Topstuff is in the process of taking legal action against Vodafone in an effort to recover losses to their business as a direct result of Vodafone's failure to secure customer information, network failures, and a new pricing model designed to attract new connections and retain existing disgruntled customers. The pricing model effectively halved Topstuff's income overnight, making it very difficult to sustain their business model.

Diagram 16 A demonstrates the mobile telecommunications market has seen the value in what Topstuff has achieved with their keyword domain names and Google page-one rankings and are now following On the Mark Marketing's initiatives with other keyword domain name variation.

Importantly, each of the domain names owned by Topstuff is now worth several thousand dollars, compared to the $24.00 they initially paid.

Bloodstone Pty Ltd

To identify the extent of the page-one rankings for all the keywords on the following domain names, I ran a search engine ranking report.

www.bloodstone.net.au
www.business-expense-analysts.com.au
www.businessexpensemanagement.com.au
www.cost-reduction-analysts.com.au
www.expense-reduction-analysts.com.au
www.procurementresource.com.au

The report showed a total of thirty-eight (38) top-ten, page-one rankings for the nine (9) keywords on these websites (see Diagram 17).

Report Overview

Date Friday, 25 March 2011

9 keywords and 6 URLs have been checked on 9 search engines The first 10 result pages of each search engine have been checked

This table lists the found rankings for all analyzed search terms, URLs and search engines

Listings in the first position	6
Listings in the top 5 positions	21
Listings in the top 10 positions	38
Listings in the top 20 positions	55
Listings in the top 30 positions	65
Total listings	91

Diagram 17

From the three examples shown, you can see how the purchase of multiple domain names incorporating keywords from the keyword research have secured multiple page-one rankings on all the major search engines. Importantly, all of these ranking will be maintained for decades, given that search engines' fundamental design is to display domain names that are searched and, secondly, where the domain name incorporates the use of keywords.

It is interesting also that in a number of instances, this domain name URL concept has gained a higher page-one ranking for the distributor than the principal.

Finally, I feel compelled to mention the three page-one rankings that were achieved for On the Mark Marketing for the keyword phrase "rapid business builders" for two websites and one domain name with a 301 redirection. This level of page-one search engine saturation multiplies the chances of capturing new business opportunities and increasing website traffic flow.

Chapter Nine

YOUR STEP-BY-STEP GUIDE TO ACHIEVING A PAGE-ONE RANKING

Take time to reflect on the products and services promoted on your website, generating a handwritten list of product/service descriptions. It is very important that you try to put yourself inside the head of one of your customers and try to think what keyword they would use to find the product/service you offer.

If this is difficult, then open a web browser and navigate to Google. Start typing the keywords you feel best describes the product/service and look at the dropdown box for clues about the keyword phrases that are being displayed. Select the most logical and see what Google AdWords campaigns are displayed and the ten companies displayed in the SEO section. If you can see all of your major competitors, then you are on the right track.

Open another tab and navigate to http://www.submitexpress. com/analyzer/; enter the website of your competitor who appears in the SEO-ranked section into the URL window and click on the "submit" button. The website will display the metatags used by your competitor to secure their page-one ranking. Look for the same keyword phrase you searched for in Google and compare this to metatag data displayed in the Submit Express page.

As you can see in Diagram 18, I have performed a search for www.onthemark.com.au. The interesting part of this exercise is as you scroll down, you can see how this page has interpreted the relevance of the meta tag data from the On the Mark Marketing website to the content of the webpage. While it may not be possible to secure a hundred percent relevancy for every webpage, the higher the score, the better your SEO ranking will be.

For this reason, it would be a good idea to bookmark the http://www.submitexpress.com/analyzer/ webpage and use it from time to time to check the relevance of all the pages on your website as you advance through the process I have outlined and as you make changes to your webpages in the future.

Diagram 18

For the next part of the process, I used www.melbourneit.com.au, which is a significant player in domain names sales in Australia. Many companies offer the facility to check the availability of domain names, so find one in your city you know and trust.

If you have not performed the keyword research I outlined in an earlier chapter, you need to do this before proceeding any further.

Copy and paste one of the keyword phrases from this research, which you should have saved into an Excel spreadsheet, into the window directly below the words "search & register your domain name here," being careful to remove any spaces between the words, then click on the "search" button, as per Diagram 19.

Diagram 19

The resulting screen will show each of the primary domain name variations that are available for your proposed keyword or secondary domain name. Assuming the domain name is available, purchase it from this provider or find a domain name provider that is more reasonably priced. In Australia, one such domain name provider is www.crazydomains.com.au, which offers a two-year domain name registration for around $24. I strongly recommend that you purchase all of the primary domain name variations. The .com, .com.au, .net, and .net.au, or the equivalent in the region your business operates. The rationalization behind this suggestion is this action will stop the competition from following your actions and registering similar domain names. This is your opportunity to not just close the door on your competition, but slam the door shut, bolt, and lock it.

If the domain name is already taken, I recommend you look to add another word into the phrase and test this process again, purchasing all of the available keyword phrases.

For the sake of a few dollars, this action will lock your competitor out of the market forever.

From this point on, you have three choices. You can develop a single webpage clone of your existing website, place a 301 redirection from the new keyword domain name to a landing page on your existing website, or host the new domain name on a different service provider's network using a 301 redirection again.

For an example of these options, please visit the following websites to see the effects these options deliver to the visitor.

1. www.marketingconsultantssydney.com.au (Single page website.)
2. www.rapidbusinessbuilder.com.au (301 redirection hosted on a second server.)
3. www.onthemarkmarketing.com.au (301 redirection.)

Example one is a single-page clone of my main website. The difference is all of the links have been set to open the respective webpage on my main website in a new browser, as show in Diagram 20.

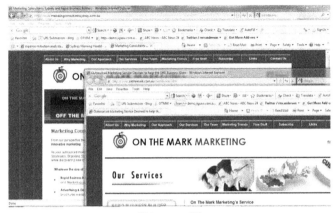

Diagram 20

The best keyword domain name to use when setting up these websites is the domain name without the "-" between the keywords and the primary domain suitable for your location. In Australia, that would be ".com.au." Use this to develop one of the options outlined earlier, then set up 301 redirections from each of the remaining domain names in this group to the specific pages on your website with the highest degree of relevance to that keyword phrase. This way, you will have multiple domain names and websites pointing to each other all using the primary keyword phrase.

The following diagram illustrates the concept behind the keyword domain names and the refinement of your current website, changing the page titles to incorporate the same keyword.

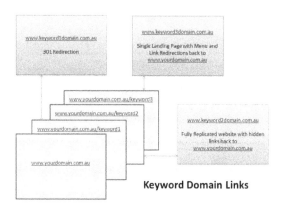

Keyword Domain Links

Diagram 21

If you don't have the skill to develop these webpages yourself, I would suggest you engage your current website developer to create one for you using a content management solution, as detailed in Chapter Five, "Search Engine Optimization."

Websites developed in this format can be copied as many times as you require, giving you the capability of creating new text for the page relevant to the keyword domain name. This way, the cost of developing multiple websites can be held to an affordable price. If, on the other hand, your company employs a full-time website development staff or outsource, the process of moving forward will be a lot simpler. I would however caution you to be prepared for an argument with your website development staff or outsource agency, which will defend the work they have performed and contest the strategy I am offering. The simple answer to this situation is, if they had thought of it first, then they would be recommending you take these actions, and if they have not, then their credibility has to be at question.

When you have developed your first keyword domain name website, you will need to find a hosting service, establish an account, and publish the website to the internet. You may need to acquire and install FTP (File Transfer Protocol) software to help manage the process of loading and, on an ongoing basis, modifying the content of the website. One of the free versions around that I like is FileZilla, which can be downloaded from http://filezilla-project.org/. Alternatively, if you have purchased an SEO software program, these products sometimes come with a built-in FTP connector.

Once you have signed up and paid for the hosting service, the hosting company will send you all the details you need to log on to your website and upload webpage content. This information will include a host IP address, user name, and password. If you are using FileZilla, simply enter these details into their respective position in your FTP application; don't put anything into the window titled port, and press the button "quick connect."

Diagram 22 shows FileZilla connected to the hosting service. Notice the application is split into five windows, the first being a display of the connectivity and confirmation you are connected to the hosting service. The next two windows in the center of the screen represent, on the left-hand side, the local directory of your computer, and on the right-hand side, the website directory you need to upload website data. You can navigate to and open any of these directories without transferring files. These windows are just a means by which you are able to see the file folder you copy from and the directory you will copy your files into. The final two windows at the bottom of the screen are, on the left-hand side, the files you need to upload, and on the right-hand side, the files you have already loaded, as is the case in this example.

Double clicking on any file in the bottom-left or right-hand windows will transfer the file into the other window. Expand the file folder titled public_html and place all the image files into the image folder, CSS files into the CSS folder and so on until all of your files have been uploaded to the host server, as shown in Diagram 22. I recommend you establish one e-mail account on each keyword domain name website and, if you are going to run multiple websites under this program, I would suggest you make the e-mail address something simple, like <u>webmaster@domain.com.au</u>, and use the same password in each instance.

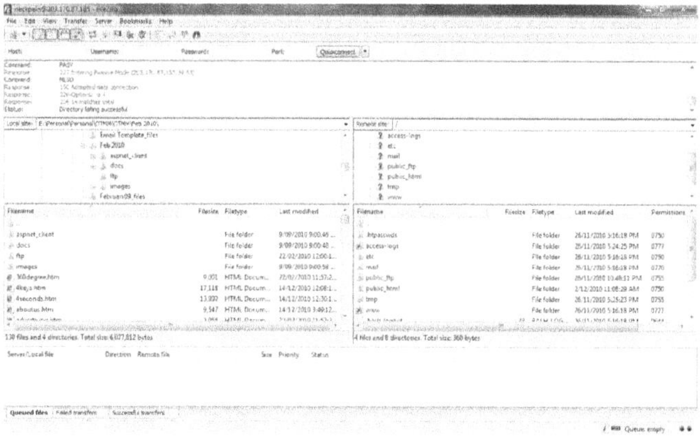

Diagram 22

Once the website has been uploaded, you will need to open an internet browser and search for the domain name to confirm the content has been published successfully. Once you have confirmed all the links are working and the website opens correctly on all pages, you will need to submit the website to the major search engines listed below. This will start the process of having your new keyword domain name website crawled by their search engine spiders for the first time.

<u>http://www.google.com.au/addurl/?continue=/addurl</u>
<u>http://www.bing.com/webmaster/SubmitSitePage.aspx</u>
<u>http://siteexplorer.search.yahoo.com/submit</u>

If you want to manage this process and extend your exposure even further, I would recommend you purchase a copy of IBP from http://www.axandra.com. This product has a search engine submission manager that can be set up to run automatically once a month, submitting all of your domain names to an extensive collection of global search engines, as shown in Diagram 23. Setting this process to run automatically will ensure your domain names are regularly updated. At a cost of US$250, the IBP standard version will let you manage this process with little ongoing involvement on your part.

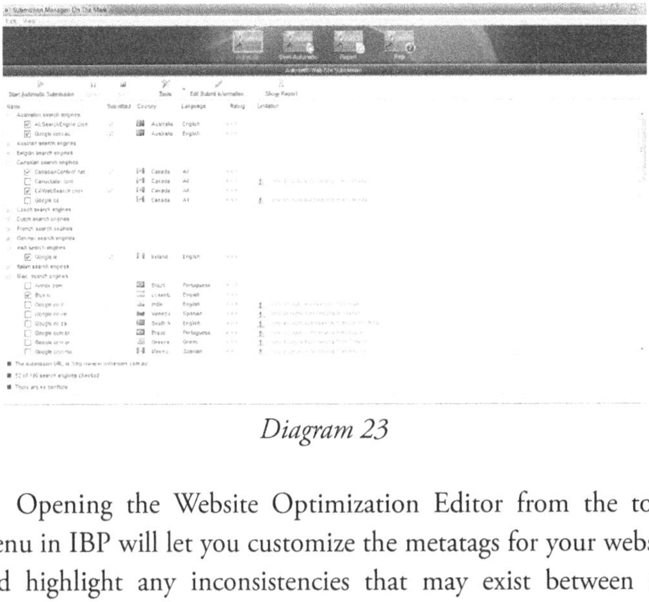

Diagram 23

Opening the Website Optimization Editor from the tools menu in IBP will let you customize the metatags for your website and highlight any inconsistencies that may exist between the metadata and the text on the respective website page. In Diagram 24, you can see the keywords for www.onthemark.com.au and the title description, along with how these compare from a quantity, density, and ranked position perspective. Small changes to the keywords used in the title will improve the relevancy of the metatags to page content. Similarly, you can make changes to the page title or page description, and add and delete keywords in these tabbed sections.

Importantly, the metatags for the webpage title, description, and keywords should be different for each page on your website. Trying to cram all of the details for your entire website into the home page is a classic mistake that is made by many website developers. Having different metadata for each page on your website will increase the relevancy of the page and ensure more of your webpages make it into the search engines database and page-one rankings.

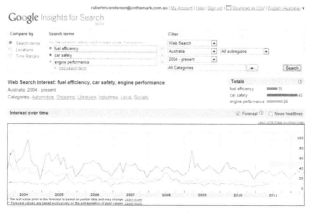

Diagram 24

Use IBP to ensure all the images on your website have alternative text names; run a full SEO report on your website, and test your ranked positions with the major search engines to measure your website's page-one ranking progress. If you have followed the guidelines and created webpages with separate metatags, the chances of these pages achieving a page-one ranking will increase significantly. Achieving a page-one ranking using a keyword domain name has incremental spinoff advantages for the content on other pages on your website.

The PageRank system used by Google increases the ranking of pages that have links to other webpages using the same keyword and hyperlinks that are already ranked highly by Google.

One amazing fact that will astonish many readers is the Google PageRank for www.marketingconsultantssydney.com.au. While this website is ranked first on page one of every search engine, the Google PageRank is 0/10. That's right—the Google PageRank does not even register this website on its radar.

There are many other things that can be done with IBP, so the best way to advance your knowledge of the product's capabilities is to download a free copy of the software and start using the product. At the very least, it will give you a better insight into how your home page is performing and what you need to do to improve its visibility on the internet.

The keyword domain name strategy outlined in the book will secure you a prominent page-one position with the major search engines within two weeks, but using a product like IBP will help perfect the work and ensure you gain even more page-one rankings for all of the pages on your websites. For me, having the first three listings on page one of Google in Australia is a fantastic achievement.

Chapter Ten

ACT NOW OR LOSE THE WAR

To put it bluntly, the domain name <u>www.googlepageoneranking.</u> <u>com.au</u>, along with all of its primary domains, can only be purchased once; I know, because I purchased the domain name. Whoever buys the keyword domain names relevant to the goods and services they sell, along with all of the primary domain variations, owns them for the rest of time. The only exception to this rule will be if the domain name holder fails to renew the domain name when it falls due for renewal or the domain name incorporates a trademark.

While it may be possible to purchase a domain name that incorporates a trademark, you will likely find the owner of the trademark would be within their rights to ask that you transfer ownership of the domain name to them.

As the old expression goes, "To the swift goes victory." The concept of keyword domain names has the potential to allow one company in every market segment to dominate their competitors by achieving multiple page-one rankings without having to pay the costs associated with pay-per-click, SEM, or SEO campaigns.

Page-one ranked positions achieved using the keyword domain names strategy will never see their page ranking position eroded by competitive SEO activity. While it is possible competitors may gain a page-one ranking using SEO techniques, the cost of achieving them in the first instance, along with the costs of maintaining the ranking, are costs the keyword domain names holder will never have to incur. Secondly, the hundreds or potentially thousands of competitors vying for one of the remaining page-one ranked positions will have to battle it out constantly for the rest of time, paying more and more every year for the privilege.

Alternatively, competitors may choose to use a PPC program to gain a sponsored advertiser's page-one ranking. The cost for this could be anywhere between $750 to several thousand dollars a month, depending on the competitive activity for keywords in your business segment.

As you work through the process, you will inevitably find some enterprising individuals have already registered domain names that are brand specific and, in some instance, keyword specific. Research suggests the people who have done this have looked at the opportunity from a single domain name perspective and have either stopped at one domain name or purchased multiple domain names and parked them for future use.

I strongly recommend you purchase multiple keyword domain names, some of which you may simply want to park, while diverting others to existing website pages with highly relevant content to the keyword using 301 redirections, and developing still others into landing pages or comprehensive webpages, depending on the volume of business these keywords could generate. It's a little like buying the land you are going to build your house on—small block, small house. Determine the size of your market from a keyword perspective, buy the land, and then build your mansion room by room.

It is all about priorities. Once you own all of the domain names from your keyword research, spilt them into groups specific to each major product/service grouping in much the same way we did with the Excel spreadsheet shown in Diagram 11, and give each group a ranked position based on its potential to give you a return on investment.

I am now and always have been an avid believer in using the profit from one marketing initiative to fund the development of other projects. So, do whatever it takes to get one keyword domain name project from each group up and running, leaving all of the other domain names parked. You can come back to these domain names later, placing 301 redirections on each keyword, or establish landing pages or websites for the others when the budget allows.

Using the keyword domain name strategy to secure page-one rankings for the hottest domain names in each group you purchased will provide the best return on your investment.

While this internet strategy will deliver a page-one ranking, it is important to note that it will take time for this initiative to gain momentum and deliver not only website traffic, but also sales to your business. Remember, cash flow is king, so give it time and just remember, if you have done your research correctly and purchased domain names wisely, you will own all the domain names in your market segment. That means you can take your time and work through the process methodically. The keyword research from Chapter Two has already confirmed what the internet-savvy public use as search terms to find the products and services you sell, so it is just a matter of time before the strategy kicks into effect.

It's important to review your keyword research every three months, purchasing additional domain names that more accurately reflect the changing landscape of your business. By doing this, you will continue to slam the door in the face of your competitors and guarantee your page-one ranking dominance.

If you have purchased a copy of IBP, then you have the tools to modify the content on your website. Using the traffic momentum from the keyword domain names and a continuing refinement of the metatags and content on each page of your website will build the page-one ranking from a single page-one ranking to multiple rankings. This will drive your competitors further down the ranked positions, onto page two and oblivion.

Just in case you haven't heard it before, let me tell you for the last time: "if you're not on page one of Google, then you're just not going to be found."

GLOSSARY

Autoresponder

An autoresponder is a computer program that automatically answers e-mail sent to it. They can be very simple or quite complex.

The first autoresponder was created within mail transfer agents that found they could not deliver an e-mail to a given address. These create bounce messages, such as "your e-mail could not be delivered because..." type responses. Today's autoresponder needs to be careful to not generate e-mail backscatter, which can result in the auto responses being considered e-mail spam.

Autoresponders are often used as e-mail marketing tools, to immediately provide information to their prospective customers and then follow up with them at pre-set time intervals.

Such *follow-up autoresponders* can be divided into two categories:

- Outsourced ASP model — these autoresponders operate on the provider's infrastructure and are usually configurable via a web-based control panel. The customer pays a monthly usage fee. This is easiest to implement for the end-user.
- Server-side — enables users to install the autoresponder system on their own server. This requires technical skills.

Autoresponders are also incorporated into electronic mailing list software to confirm subscriptions, un-subscriptions, posts, and other list activities.

Cascading Style Sheet (CSS)

CSS is a style sheet language used to describe the presentation semantics (the look and formatting) of a document written in a mark-up language. It's most common application is to style webpages written in HTML and XHTML, but the language can also be applied to any kind of XML document, including SVG and XUL.

CSS is designed primarily to enable the separation of document content (written in HTML or a similar mark-up language) from document presentation, including elements such as the layout, colors, and fonts. This separation can improve content accessibility, provide more flexibility and control in the specification of presentation characteristics, enable multiple pages to share formatting, and reduce complexity and repetition in the structural content (such as by allowing for tableless web design). CSS can also allow the same mark-up page to be presented in different styles for different rendering methods, such as on-screen, in print, by voice (when read out by a speech-based browser or screen reader), and on Braille-based, tactile devices. While the author of a document typically links that document to a CSS style sheet, readers can use a different style sheet, perhaps one on their own computer, to override the one the author has specified.

CSS specifies a priority scheme to determine which style rules apply if more than one rule matches against a particular element. In this so-called *cascade*, priorities or *weights* are calculated and assigned to rules, so that the results are predictable.

The CSS specifications are maintained by the World Wide Web Consortium (W3C). Internet media type (MIME type) text/css is registered for use with CSS by RFC 2318 (March 1998).

The popularity of CSS as a design tool has increased steadily and is now regarded as the premier system for website design.

Click Fraud

Click fraud is a type of internet crime that occurs in pay-per-click online advertising when a person, automated script, or computer program imitates a legitimate user of a web browser, clicking on an ad to generate a charge per click without having actual interest in the target of the ad's link. Click fraud is the subject of some controversy and increasing litigation due to the advertising networks being a key beneficiary of the fraud.

Use of a computer to commit this type of internet fraud is a felony in many jurisdictions. There have been arrests relating to click fraud with regard to malicious clicking in order to deplete a competitor's advertising budget

Click Through Rate (CTR)

Click Through Rate or CTR is a way of measuring the success of an online advertising campaign. A CTR is obtained by dividing the "number of users who clicked on an ad" on a webpage by the "number of times the ad was delivered" (impressions). For example, if a banner ad was delivered one hundred times (impressions delivered) and one person clicked on it (clicks recorded), then the resulting CTR would be one percent.

Banner ad click-through rates have fallen over time; when they first started to appear, it was not uncommon to have rates above five percent. They have fallen since then, currently averaging closer to 0.2 or 0.3 percent. In most cases, a two percent click-through rate would be considered very successful, though the exact number is hotly debated and would vary depending on the situation. The average click-through rate of three percent in the 1990s declined to 0.28 percent by 2003. Since advertisers typically pay more for a high click-through rate, getting many click-throughs with few purchases is undesirable to advertisers. Similarly, by selecting an appropriate advertising site with high affinity (e.g., a movie magazine for a movie advertisement), the same banner can achieve a substantially higher CTR. Personalized ads, unusual formats, and more obtrusive ads typically have higher click-through rates than standard banner ads; however, overly intrusive ads are often avoided by viewers.

CTR is most commonly defined as "number of clicks" divided by "number of impressions," and generally, not in terms of the "number of persons" who clicked divided by the "number of impressions." This is an important distinction. As a person clicks a single advertisement multiple times, the CTR increases using the former definition, whereas the CTR does not change using the latter definition.

Cost Per Click (CPC)

Pay per click (PPC) is an internet advertising model used on websites, where advertisers pay their host only when their ad is clicked. With search engines, advertisers typically bid on keyword phrases relevant to their target market. Content sites commonly charge a fixed price per click rather than use a bidding system.

Cost per click (CPC) is the sum paid by an advertiser to search engines and other internet publishers for a single click on their advertisement, which directs one visitor to the advertiser's website.

In contrast to the generalized portal, which seeks to drive a high volume of traffic to one site, PPC implements the so-called affiliate model that provides purchase opportunities wherever people may be surfing. It does this by offering financial incentives (in the form of a percentage of revenue) to affiliated partner sites. The affiliates provide purchase-point click-through to the merchant. It is a pay-for-performance model: if an affiliate does not generate sales, it represents no cost to the merchant. Variations include banner exchange, pay-per-click, and revenue-sharing programs.

Websites that utilize PPC ads will display an advertisement when a keyword query matches an advertiser's keyword list, or when a content site displays relevant content. Such advertisements are called *sponsored links* or *sponsored ads*, and appear adjacent to or above organic results on search-engine-results pages, or anywhere a web developer chooses on a content site.

Among PPC providers, Google AdWords, Yahoo! Search Marketing, and Microsoft adCenter are the three largest network operators, and all three operate under a bid-based model. Cost per click (CPC) varies depending on the search engine and the level of competition for a particular keyword.

The PPC advertising model is open to abuse through click fraud, although Google and others have implemented automated systems to guard against abusive clicks by competitors or corrupt web developers.

Damping Factor

The term damping factor can also refer to the amount of damping in any oscillatory system or in numerical algorithms.

In audio system terminology, the **damping factor** gives the ratio of the rated impedance of the loudspeaker to the source impedance. Only the resistive part of the loudspeaker impedance is used. The amplifier output impedance is also assumed to be totally resistive. The source impedance (that seen by the loudspeaker) includes the connecting cable impedance.

Eigengap

In linear algebra, the eigengap of a linear operator is the difference between two successive eigenvalues, where eigenvalues are sorted in ascending order.

The Davis–Kahan theorem, named after Chandler Davis and William Kahan, uses the eigengap to show how eigenspaces of an operator change under perturbation. In spectral clustering, the eigengap is often referred to as the *spectral gap,* although the spectral gap may often be defined in a broader sense than that of the eigengap.

H1 Heading Tags

In writing structured documents, the focus is on encoding the logical structure of a document, with no explicit concern in the structural mark-up for its presentation to humans by printed pages, screens, or other means. Structured documents, especially well formed ones, can easily be processed by computer systems to extract and present metadata about the document. In most Wikipedia articles, for example, a table of contents is automatically generated from the different heading tags in the body of the document. Popular word processors can have such a function available.

In HTML, a part of the logical structure of a document may be the document body,<body>, containing a first level heading,<h1>, and a paragraph,<p>.

```
<body>
<h1>Structured document</h1>
<p>A <strong class="selflink">structured document</strong> is an <a href="/Electronic_document" title="Electronic document">electronic document</a> where some method of <a href="/w/index.php?title=Embedded_coding&action=edit&redlink=1"
```

class="new" title="Embedded coding (page does not exist)">embedded coding</a>, such as <a href="/Markup_language" title="Markup language">markup</a>, is used to give the whole, and parts, of the document various structural meanings according to a <a href="/Schema" title="Schema">schema</a>.</P>

</body>

The HTML coding shown above would be displayed in a web browser the following way.

Structured Document

A **structured document** is an electronic document where some method of embedded coding, such as mark-up, is used to give the whole, and parts, of the document various structural meanings according to a schema.

Landing Page

In online marketing, a landing page, sometimes known as a lead capture page, is a single webpage that appears in response to clicking on an advertisement. The landing page will usually display directed sales copy that is a logical extension of the advertisement or link.

Landing pages are often linked to from social media, e-mail campaigns, or pay per click (PPC) campaigns in order to enhance the effectiveness of the advertisements. The general goal of a landing page is to convert site visitors into sales leads. By studying metrics or analytics of the linking URL, marketers can compare the click-through rates and conversion rate to determine the most profitable advertisement.

Meta Tags

Meta elements are the HTML or XHTML <meta … > element used to provide structured metadata about a webpage. Multiple elements are often used on the same page: the element is the same, but its attributes are different. Meta elements can be used to specify page description, keywords, and any other metadata not provided through the other head elements and attributes.

The meta element has two uses: either to emulate the use of the HTTP response header or to embed additional metadata within the HTML document. There are four valid attributes: content, http-equiv, name, and scheme. http-equiv is used to emulate the HTTP header. The value of the statement, in either case, is contained in the content attribute, which is the only required attribute.

Such elements must be placed as tags in the head section of an HTML or XHTML document.

Metadata

Metadata is loosely defined as data about data. Metadata is traditionally found in the card catalogues of libraries. By describing the contents and context of data files, the quality of the original data/files is greatly increased. For example, a webpage may include metadata specifying what language it's written in, what tools were used to create it, and where to go for more on the subject, allowing browsers to automatically improve the experience of users.

Outdegree

For a node, the number of head endpoints adjacent to a node is called the indegree of the node and the number of tail endpoints is its outdegree.

The indegree is denoted deg $^-$ (v) and the outdegree as deg $^+$ (v). A vertex with deg $^-$ (v) = 0 is called a source, as it is the origin of each of its incident edges. Similarly, a vertex with deg $^+$ (v) = 0 is called a sink.

PageRank

PageRank is a link analysis algorithm named after Larry Page and used by the Google Internet search engine that assigns a numerical weighting to each element of a hyperlinked set of documents, such as the World Wide Web, with the purpose of "measuring" its relative importance within the set. The algorithm may be applied to any collection of entities with reciprocal quotations and references. The numerical weight that it assigns to any given element E is referred to as the *PageRank of E* and denoted by $PR(E)$.

The name "PageRank" is a trademark of Google, and the PageRank process has been patented (U.S. Patent 6,285,999). However, the patent is assigned to Stanford University and not to Google. Google has exclusive license rights on the patent from Stanford University. The university received 1.8 million shares of Google in exchange for use of the patent; the shares were sold in 2005 for $336 million.

Perron-Frobenius

In linear algebra, the Perron–Frobenius theorem, proved by Oskar Perron (1907) and Georg Frobenius (1912), asserts that a real square matrix with positive entries has a unique largest real eigenvalue and that the corresponding eigenvector has strictly positive components, and also asserts a similar statement for certain classes of nonnegative matrices. This theorem has important applications to probability theory (ergodicity of Markov chains); to the theory of dynamical systems (sub shifts of finite type); to economics (Leontief's input-output model); to demography (Leslie population age distribution model); to mathematical background of the internet search engines; and even to ranking of football teams.

Pay Per Click (PPC)

Pay per click (PPC) is an internet advertising model used on websites, where advertisers pay their host only when their ad is clicked. With search engines, advertisers typically bid on keyword phrases relevant to their target market. Content sites commonly charge a fixed price per click rather than use a bidding system.

Cost per click (CPC) is the sum paid by an advertiser to search engines and other internet publishers for a single click on their advertisement, which directs one visitor to the advertiser's website.

In contrast to the generalized portal, which seeks to drive a high volume of traffic to one site, PPC implements the so-called affiliate model that provides purchase opportunities wherever people may be surfing. It does this by offering financial incentives (in the form of a percentage of revenue) to affiliated partner sites. The affiliates provide purchase-point click-through to the merchant. It is a pay-for-performance model: if an affiliate does not generate sales, it represents no cost to the merchant. Variations include banner exchange, pay-per-click, and revenue-sharing programs.

Websites that utilize PPC ads will display an advertisement when a keyword query matches an advertiser's keyword list, or when a content site displays relevant content. Such advertisements are called *sponsored links* or *sponsored ads*, and appear adjacent to or above organic results on search engine results pages, or anywhere a web developer chooses on a content site.

Among PPC providers, Google AdWords, Yahoo! Search Marketing, and Microsoft adCenter are the three largest network operators, and all three operate under a bid-based model. Cost per click (CPC) varies depending on the search engine and the level of competition for a particular keyword.

The PPC advertising model is open to abuse through click fraud, although Google and others have implemented automated systems to guard against abusive clicks by competitors or corrupt web developers.

RSS

RSS (most commonly expanded as Really Simple Syndication) is a family of web feed formats used to publish frequently updated works—such as blog entries, news headlines, audio, and video—in a standardized format. An RSS document (which is called a "feed," "web feed," or "channel") includes full or summarized text, plus metadata, such as publishing dates and authorship. Web feeds benefit publishers by letting them syndicate content automatically. They benefit readers who want to subscribe to timely updates from favored websites or to aggregate feeds from many sites into one place. RSS feeds can be read using software called an "RSS reader," "feed reader," or "aggregator," which can be web-based, desktop-based, or mobile-device-based. A standardized XML file format allows the information to be published once and viewed by many different programs. The user subscribes to a feed by entering into the reader the feed's URL or by clicking a icon in a web browser, which initiates the subscription process. The RSS reader checks the user's subscribed feeds regularly for new work, downloads any updates that it finds, and provides a user interface to monitor and read the feeds. RSS allows users to avoid manually inspecting all of the websites they are interested in, and instead subscribe to many websites such that all new content is pushed onto their browsers when it becomes available.

RSS formats are specified using XML, a generic specification for the creation of data formats. Although RSS formats have evolved from as early as March 1999, it was between 2005 and 2006, when RSS gained widespread use, and the RSS icon was decided upon by several major web browsers.

Search Engine Robots or Search Engine Spider or Web Crawler

Web crawler is a computer program that browses the World Wide Web in a methodical, automated manner or in an orderly fashion. Other terms for web crawlers are *ants*, *automatic indexers*, *bots*, *web spiders*, *web robots*, or—especially in the FOAF community—*web scutters*.

This process is called *web crawling* or *spidering*. Many sites, in particular search engines, use spidering as a means of providing up-to-date data. Web crawlers are mainly used to create a copy of all the visited pages for later processing by a search engine that will index the downloaded pages to provide fast searches. Crawlers can also be used for automating maintenance tasks on a website, such as checking links or validating HTML code. In addition, crawlers can be used to gather specific types of information from webpages, such as harvesting e-mail addresses (usually for spam).

A web crawler is one type of bot or software agent. In general, it starts with a list of URLs to visit, called the *seeds*. As the crawler visits these URLs, it identifies all the hyperlinks in the page and adds them to the list of URLs to visit, called the *crawl frontier*. URLs from the frontier are recursively visited according to a set of policies.

SEM

Search engine marketing, or SEM, is a form of internet marketing that seeks to promote websites by increasing their visibility in search engine result pages (SERPs) with search engine optimization, paid placement, contextual advertising, and paid inclusion.

Search Engine Optimization (SEO)

Search engine optimization (SEO) is the process of improving the visibility of a website or a webpage in search engines via the "natural" or un-paid ("organic" or "algorithmic") search results. Other forms of search engine marketing (SEM) like Google AdWords are ranked by how much the advertiser is prepared to pay. In general, the earlier (or higher on the page) and more frequently a site appears in the search results list, the more visitors it will receive from the search engine. SEO may target different kinds of searches, including image search, local search, video search, and industry-specific vertical search engines. This gives a website web presence.

As an internet marketing strategy, SEO considers how search engines work and what people search for when they use search engines. Optimizing a website may involve editing its content and HTML and associated coding to both increase its relevance to specific keywords and to remove barriers to the indexing activities of search engines. Promoting a site to increase the number of backlinks, or inbound links, is another SEO tactic.

The acronym "SEO" can refer to "search engine optimizers," a term adopted by an industry of consultants who carry out optimization projects on behalf of clients, and by employees who perform SEO services in-house. Search engine optimizers may offer SEO as a stand-alone service or as a part of a broader marketing campaign. Because effective SEO may require changes to the HTML source code of a site and site content, SEO tactics may be incorporated into website development and design. The term "search engine friendly" may be used to describe website designs, menus, content management systems, images, videos, shopping carts, and other elements that have been optimized for the purpose of search engine exposure.

SERP Rank

The search engine results page (SERP) is the actual result returned by a search engine in response to a keyword query. The SERP consists of a list of links to webpages with associated text snippets. The SERP rank of a webpage refers to the placement of the corresponding link on the SERP, where higher placement means higher SERP rank. The SERP rank of a webpage is not only a function of its PageRank, but depends on a relatively large and continuously adjusted set of factors (over 200), commonly referred to by internet marketers as "Google Love." Search engine optimization (SEO) is aimed at achieving the highest possible SERP rank for a website or a set of webpages.

With the introduction of Google Places into the mainstream organic SERP, PageRank plays little to no role in ranking a business in the local business results. While the theory of citations is still computed in their algorithm, PageRank is not a factor, since Google ranks business listings and not webpages.

Spamdexing

Spamdexing (also known as search spam, search engine spam, or web spam) involves a number of methods, such as repeating unrelated phrases, to manipulate the relevance or prominence of resources indexed by a search engine, in a manner inconsistent with the purpose of the indexing system. Some consider it a part of search engine optimization, though there are many search engine optimization methods that improve the quality and appearance of the content of web sites and serve content useful to many users. Search engines use a variety of algorithms to determine relevancy ranking. Some of these include determining whether the search term appears in the META keywords tag, others whether the search term appears in the body text or URL of a webpage. Many search engines check for instances of spamdexing and will remove suspect pages from their indexes. In addition, people working for a search-engine organization can quickly block the results listing from entire websites that use spamdexing, perhaps alerted by user complaints of false matches. The rise of spamdexing in the mid-1990s made the leading search engines of the time less useful.

Spoofing

Website spoofing is the act of creating a website, as a hoax, with the intention of misleading readers that the website has been created by a different person or organization. Another meaning for spoof is fake websites. Normally, the website will adopt the design of the target website and sometimes has a similar URL.

Another technique is to use a cloaked URL. By using domain forwarding, or inserting control characters, the URL can appear to be genuine while concealing the address of the actual website.

The objective may be fraudulent, often associated with phishing or e-mail spoofing, or to criticize or make fun of the person or body whose website the spoofed site purports to represent.

As an example of the use of this technique to parody an organization, in November 2006 two spoof websites were produced claiming that Microsoft had bought Firefox and released Microsoft Firefox 2007.

LIST OF DIAGRAMS

Diagram 1 shows how the metatag description is displayed as part of the listing on the Google Search Engine results screen for the keyword phrase "rapid business builder."

Diagram 2 shows how the metatag title is displayed in the tab at the top of Internet Explorer page.

Diagram 3 shows part one of the Google AdWords screen and the use of the keyword research tool.

Diagram 4 shows part two of the Google AdWords screen and the use of the download facility of this keyword research tool.

Diagram 5 illustrates that between 2004 and the present day car safety ranks high in the consumers' mind followed by engine performance and last of all fuel efficiency.

Diagram 6 illustrates a notable shift in the importance of keywords when I change the time filter from 2004 to the present day, to the last 12-months.

Diagram 7 shows a pattern of interest over all the states of Australia for Fuel Efficiency.

Diagram 8 shows a pattern of interest over all the states of Australia for Car Safety.

Diagram 9 shows a pattern of interest over all the states of Australia for Engine Performance.

Diagram 10 shows the drop down selection box for search terms used for each of the search terms that will allow you to see the keyword searched for under fuel efficiency, car safety, or engine performance.

Diagram 11 shows an Excel spreadsheet used to separate keywords into logical Google AdWords groupings and the advertisement created for them.

Diagram 12 shows top nine SEO software solutions and links to the products review.

Diagram 13 shows Google search results for "rapid business builders" (pages from Australia), with the first three listings all being owned by On the Mark Marketing.

Diagram 14 shows all three page-one rankings owned by On the Mark Marketing Pty Ltd.

Diagram 15 shows the Page Rank Report for On the Mark Marketing Pty Ltd.

Diagram 16 A shows Topstuff Pty Ltd have outranked the top three Telco's in Australia.

Diagram 16 A demonstrates the telecommunications market in Australia has seen the value of using the DNO Strategy in domain names.

Diagram 16 B shows the Page Rank Report for Topstuff Pty Ltd.

Diagram 17 shows the Page Rank Report for Bloodstone Pty Ltd.

Diagram 18 shows the use of Submit Express website to check the metadata for On the Mark Marketing or any website comparing the website's relevance to the page title, page description, and keywords.

Diagram 19 shows the use of the www.melbourneit.com.au website to search for available keyword domain names developed from keyword research.

Diagram 20 shows the results of clicking on a link from a single webpage website that opens the respective page on another website in a new browser window.

Diagram 21 illustrates the concept behind the keyword domain names and the refinement of your current website, changing the page titles to incorporate the same keyword.

Diagram 22 shows the use of the FTP software called FileZilla to upload new content to a website.

Diagram 23 shows the IBP Search Engine Submission Screen.

Diagram 24 shows the IBP SEO program and its Website Optimization Tools menu to customize the metatags for your website and highlight inconsistencies between the metadata and the webpage content.

BIBLIOGRAPHY

1. Autoresponder. "Wikipedia"
   Last Modified November 14, 2010
   http://en.wikipedia.org/wiki/Autoresponder

2. Cascading Style Sheets. "Wikipedia"
   Last Modified April 4, 2011
   http://en.wikipedia.org/wiki/Cascading_Style_Sheet

3. Click Fraud. "Wikipedia"
   Last Modified April 4, 2011
   http://en.wikipedia.org/wiki/Click_fraud

4. Click Through Rate. "Wikipedia"
   Last Modified February 15, 2011
   http://en.wikipedia.org/wiki/Click_Through_Rate

5. Damping Factor. "Wikipedia"
   Last Modified March 23, 2011
   http://en.wikipedia.org/wiki/Damping_factor

6. Eigengap. "Wikipedia"
   Last Modified April 11, 2010
   http://en.wikipedia.org/wiki/Eigengap

7.   Google Annual Revenue. "Fourth Quarter and Fiscal Year 2009 Results."
      January 21, 2010
      http://investor.google.com/earnings/2009/Q4_google_earnings.html

8.   Google Market Share by Competitor. Google Market Share"
      Last modified February 10, 2010
      http://www.getclickz.com/2010/02/10/search-engine-market-share-3/

9.   Google Market Share by Country. "Google System Blogspot,"
      Last modifiedMarch3, 2009
      http://googlesystem.blogspot.com/2009/03/googles-market-share-in-your-country.html.

10.   Google PageRank Algorithms. "Wikipedia"
      Last modified March 23, 2011
      http://en.wikipedia.org/wiki/PageRank.

11.   Google Adwords. "Google"
      Last modified 2011
      https://adwords.google.com.au

12.   Google Insight. "Google"
      Last modified 2011
      http://www.google.com/insights/search

13.   H1 Heading Tags. "Wikipedia"
      Last Modified February 11, 2011
      http://en.wikipedia.org/wiki/Structured_document

14. Landing Page. "Wikipedia"
     Last Modified March 22, 2011
     http://en.wikipedia.org/wiki/Landing_Page

15. Metadata. "Wikipedia"
     Last Modified March 22, 2011
     http://en.wikipedia.org/wiki/Metadata

16. Meta Tags. "Wikipedia"
     Last Modified April 1, 2011
     http://en.wikipedia.org/wiki/Meta_tags

17. Outdegree. "Wikipedia"
     Last Modified April 3, 2011
     http://en.wikipedia.org/wiki/Outdegree#Indegree_and_outdegree

18. PageRank. "Wikipedia"
     Last Modified April 2, 2011
     http://en.wikipedia.org/wiki/PageRank

19. Pay Per Click (PPC). "Wikipedia"
     Last Modified March 27, 2011
     http://en.wikipedia.org/wiki/Pay_per_click

20. Pay Per Click. "Wikipedia"
     Last Modified May 18, 2010
     http://en.wikipedia.org/wiki/Cost_Per_Click

21. Perron-Frobenius. "Wikipedia"
     Last Modified April 5, 2011
     http://en.wikipedia.org/wiki/Perron%E2%80%93Frobenius_theorem

22. RSS. "Wikipedia"
Last Modified February 3, 2011
http://en.wikipedia.org/wiki/RSS

23. SEO Software Review. "SEO Software Review Top Ten Reviews"
Accessed April 5, 2011
http://seo-software-review.toptenreviews.com

24. SEO. "Wikipedia"
Last Modified April 1, 2011
http://en.wikipedia.org/wiki/SEO

25. Search Engine Robots or Search Engine Spider or Web Crawler. "Wikipedia"
Last Modified April 4, 2011
http://en.wikipedia.org/wiki/Web_crawler

26. SEM. "Wikipedia"
Last Modified April 1, 2011
http://en.wikipedia.org/wiki/Search_engine_marketing

27. SERP Rank. "Wikipedia"
Last Modified February 16, 2011
http://en.wikipedia.org/wiki/Search_engine_results_page

28. Spamdexing. "Wikipedia"
Last Modified April 3, 2011
http://en.wikipedia.org/wiki/Spamdexing

29. Spoofing. "Wikipedia"
Last Modified March 16, 2011
http://en.wikipedia.org/wiki/Website_spoofing

30. U.S. Search Engine Rankings. "comScore Media Release"
     August, 2010
     http://comscore.com/Press_Events/Press_Releases/2010/9/
     comScore_Releases_August_2010_U.S._Search_Engine_
     Rankings

31. Vodafone losing 100,000 customers per month. "Sydney
     Morning Herald"
     Last Modified May 5, 2011
     http://www.smh.com.au/business/vodafones-losses-are-
     telstras-gains-20110504-1e8k5.html

32. Webmaster Guidelines Google. "Google"
     Accessed March20, 2011
     http://www.google.com/support/webmasters/bin/answer.
     py?answer=35769

INDEX

ABOUT THE AUTHOR

Robert is a senior partner in a small marketing services company located in Sydney, Australia, specializing in outsourced marketing services and strategy development for SME (small medium enterprise) businesses.

His investigation into the search engine visibility of thousands of websites has confirmed website owners, developers, copywriters, graphic designers, SEO and SEM experts in the great majority of instances are incapable of working together cohesively. This knowledge led Robert to the development of a unique internet strategy that will make current SEO techniques obsolete and deliver sustainable page-one rankings for less than $100.

Robert is a former winner of the prestigious Australian Sales Manager of the Year, having been recognized for his ability to motivate salespeople, the creation of innovative incentive plans, exceeding sales forecast, and the use of technology designed to reduce sales cycles.

He gained his skill and knowledge working in senior sales and marketing roles with 3M, Canon, Expertise Events, Intercept Information Solutions, Grace Imaging Solutions, and On the Mark Marketing.

A founding publisher and editor of Australia's first imaging magazine, *Image and Data Manager*, and past national president of IIM (Institute of Image Management), Robert played a prominent role in developing media communications, conferences, and exhibitions that focused on document imaging and knowledge management solutions.

In recognition of his contribution to the document imaging market, he was made a fellow of AIIM (Association for Information and Image Management) USA and is the only Australian to have been acknowledged in this way.

BUY A SHARE OF THE FUTURE IN YOUR COMMUNITY

These certificates make great holiday, graduation and birthday gifts that can be personalized with the recipient's name. The cost of one S.H.A.R.E. or one square foot is $54.17. The personalized certificate is suitable for framing and will state the number of shares purchased and the amount of each share, as well as the recipient's name. The home that you participate in "building" will last for many years and will continue to grow in value.

Here is a sample SHARE certificate:

HABITAT FOR HUMANITY

THIS CERTIFIES THAT

YOUR NAME HERE

HAS INVESTED IN A HOME FOR A DESERVING FAMILY

1985-2010

TWENTY-FIVE YEARS OF BUILDING FUTURES
IN OUR COMMUNITY ONE HOME AT A TIME

1200 SQUARE FOOT HOUSE @ $65,000 = $54.17 PER SQUARE FOOT
This certificate represents a tax deductible donation. It has no cash value.

YES, I WOULD LIKE TO HELP!

*I support the work that Habitat for Humanity does and I want to be part of the excitement! As a donor, I will receive periodic updates on your construction activities but, more importantly, I know my gift will help a family in our community realize the dream of homeownership. **I would like to SHARE in your efforts against substandard housing in my community!*** (Please print below)

PLEASE SEND ME _____ SHARES at $54.17 EACH = $ $_____

In Honor Of: _____

Occasion: (Circle One)   HOLIDAY   BIRTHDAY   ANNIVERSARY

OTHER: _____

Address of Recipient: _____

Gift From: _____ *Donor Address:* _____

Donor Email: _____

I AM ENCLOSING A CHECK FOR $ $_____ PAYABLE TO HABITAT FOR HUMANITY **OR** PLEASE CHARGE MY VISA OR MASTERCARD *(CIRCLE ONE)*

Card Number _____ Expiration Date: _____

Name as it appears on Credit Card _____ Charge Amount $ _____

Signature _____

Billing Address _____

Telephone # Day _____ Eve _____

PLEASE NOTE: Your contribution is tax-deductible to the fullest extent allowed by law.
Habitat for Humanity • P.O. Box 1443 • Newport News, VA 23601 • 757-596-5553
www.HelpHabitatforHumanity.org